JAPAN AND KOREA:

America's Allies
In the Pacific

THE WALKER SUMMIT LIBRARY NO. 5

JAPAN AND KOREA:

America's Allies
In the Pacific

James W. Morley
Columbia University

WALKER AND COMPANY New York

PREFACE

In Northeast Asia, where we have been drawn into war twice in the past generation, our allies in Japan and South Korea confront a massive challenge from the Communist-organized Russians, Chinese and North Koreans. At the same time, they are at least equally challenged by a host of other problems. The Japanese are assaulting the final peaks in their dramatic climb to prosperity and modernity, to democratic stability, and to a new position of independence and influence in the world. The South Koreans, on the other hand, are still striving to find their way out of the age-old valleys of hunger, violence and insecurity while cut off from their compatriots to the North. We Americans are deeply involved in these problems, for their outcome will have a profound effect, not only on the Japanese and Koreans themselves, but on us and all the rest of the world as well. It is important therefore that we try to understand them better.

This volume is in two parts. The first part consists of three essays in which are discussed the evolving domestic political situation in contemporary Japan and Korea, and the trends and problems of the foreign relations of each, with particular reference to their relations with each other and to the problems they present to American policy. It is hoped that these essays will provide some explanation of the roads already taken and some background against which to judge the events yet to unfold. The second part is an appendix of useful political, economic and cultural information in tabular form for reference; it was prepared with the help of Mr. Sung-hwan Chang.

J. W. M.

CONTENTS

Part I: Interpretation

Part II: Reference

Part One: INTERPRETATION

Section One CONSERVATIVE JAPAN

I. CAUTION ABROAD

The San Francisco Peace Treaty, which restored Japan to legal independence in 1952, has been widely heralded in this country as a treaty of reconciliation. It was indeed "softer" than the settlement most Americans had envisioned when the war ended in 1945. Some Americans had talked then of occupying Japan for twenty years or more, removing its industrial plants to the lands of the victors, limiting its economy to subsistence agriculture, and placing it under international surveillance for a long time to come.

However, by 1950, when peace treaty negotiations began in earnest, the American attitude had softened. Much has been said about the effect of the Occupation on the Japanese. The effect on the Americans was also profound. By bringing Americans into prolonged personal contact with their former enemy and by imposing on them direct responsibility for Japan's problems, the Occupation gradually eroded many of the war-engendered hates and fears, and replaced them with sympathy. At the same time, the chilling of U.S.–Soviet relations, the take-over of China by the Communists, and the outbreak of the Korean war all served to persuade the United States that the chief threat to its security was not the enemy of the past, but the Communists of the present. Consequently, America shifted its strategy from suppressing Japan to rehabilitating it, from forcing Japan to beat its swords into plowshares to encouraging it to remold its swords and persuading it to use them in the service of its own independence and the vast international coalition being built against the Communist powers.

In the treaty negotiations, therefore, America insisted that reparations should be left for future determination, that the continuation of Occupation reforms should be left to the judgment of the Japanese people, and that the right to rearm should be returned unimpaired. Thus, compared with the settlement that had once been anticipated, the Japanese peace treaty was "soft" indeed.

Most of our friends and allies thought America extremely unwise. The tiger, they said, had not changed its stripes. The United States might be ready to forgive and forget, but the Japanese were not. They would not be reconciled by a "soft" treaty. Unless held in check, as soon as the opportunity presented itself, they would revoke their new constitution, rebuild their armed forces, and set out belligerently to revise the postwar settlement; they would resume their drive to dominate Asia.

This fear was understandable, for, in spite of the relative "softness" of the Treaty, the total settlement, if the Occupation reforms are included, was as harsh as that experienced by any major power in modern times. Occupied for seven years by victorious powers, Japan was compelled to change its social and economic structure, reorganize its government, reorient its educational system, renounce its national beliefs and patriotic loyalties, repatriate its people and abandon its sovereignty over an empire parts of which, like Taiwan, it had held for more than fifty years, and still other parts of which, like the southern Kurile, the Ryukyu and the Bonin Islands, it had considered part of the homeland throughout modern times. In addition, it was forced to disband its armed forces, so that it could not even protect what was left of its territory without permitting the former principal occupying power to retain military bases on its soil.

Suppose we had lost the war and, as a consequence, had been subjected to a similar settlement. One supposes instinctively that, as soon as possible, we would have repledged ourselves to our traditional values, striven to overturn the "reforms" and restore our traditional institutions, and worked unceasingly to revive the power and prestige of an independent America in the world. Many of our foreign friends and allies, reflecting on their own imagined feelings under similar circumstances and judging from the history of Germany and Italy following World War I, were sure in 1952 that the Japanese people would react in the same way, that, once the restraints of the Occupation were lifted, they would revert to their prewar and wartime policies.

3

The striking fact is that neither the prediction of America nor that of the Allies has proved wholly accurate. Japan has not become the belligerent, revisionist power feared by the Allies. It has retained its new Constitution, raised economic administrators rather than demagogues to power, preferred butter to guns, and sought markets, not colonies or bases. In short, it has pursued a foreign policy of economic strength and political reconciliation.

In line with America's hopes, it has remained friendly to us, has in fact become our second-most-important trading partner, has cooperated militarily by allowing American troops to continue to use Japan as a base, and has been generally amenable to American leadership in foreign policy. On the other hand, it has not responded to the Treaty with the enthusiasm and vigor that the United States really anticipated and desired. It did not leap at the opportunity to rearm as American officials expected. It has in fact been extremely slow to rearm and even today commits a smaller percentage of its gross national product and national budget to military expenses than any other power of similar potential. It has permitted informal trading and personal exchanges with Communist China, and many of its leaders have expressed such sympathy with the Communist Chinese that the pull toward China has become a constant irritant in Japanese-American relations. In the underdeveloped parts of the world, particularly South and Southeast Asia, it has been much slower to accept any real responsibility than had been hoped. In short, it has not overnight become a dynamic center of "free world" power in Asia, but rather a cautious friend who cultivates his own garden.

Limited Rearmament and the Security Treaty

Since 1952, Japan has sought to defend herself militarily by pursuing a dual policy of limited rearmament and alliance with the United States. Consistently since 1950, when the National Police Reserve was formed, the Japanese conservative leaders have felt that Japan must rebuild her armed forces; but they have not thought it either desirable or possible to revive the wartime and prewar goals of strength sufficient to take on all comers in Asia. Instead, they have pursued a policy of gradual, limited rearmament in accord with five major determinants: the nation's economic means, the will of

4

the Japanese people, the tolerance of the powers, the demands of the United States, and the advancement of technology.

There is, of course, no generally accepted formula to determine what percentage of a nation's gross national product can be devoted to military purposes without weakening the economy. Nevertheless, it is clear that in Japan the percentage that has been so used has, at less than 2.5 per cent, been extraordinarily low. The fact that the government has refused to raise this level, in spite of strong and repeated pressure from the United States, testifies clearly to the primacy of its policy of butter—or, more accurately, of rice.

This low level of expenditure reflects also the great sensitivity of postwar Japanese governments to the will of the people. For many reasons, partly from disillusionment following defeat in the war, partly from fear of a revival of domestic military influence, and partly from the official pacifism of the Occupation, which was written into the ban on "war potential" in Article IX of the Constitution, rearmament has been very unpopular in Japan. Most Japanese are prepared to accept some arms as a matter of necessity, but they do so reluctantly and want them strictly limited. In turn the progressive political parties of the Left have been able to exploit this pacifist sentiment sufficiently to convince the government that it must proceed with great caution lest it be voted out of power.

The government is also deeply conscious of the fears and hatreds still harbored by many of the peoples that Japan overran in its struggle to build a Greater East Asia; and it is no less sensitive to the effect even limited rearmament has on the attitudes and policies of its powerful Communist neighbors. These factors, however, it has had to balance against the opposite pressures emanating from the United States, whose military and economic aid Japan has been anxious to maximize.

Finally, changes in military technology since the war have created problems for the Japanese as for all peoples. The advent of perfected radar, nuclear warheads, jet propulsion and the whole developing range of modern weapons has drastically altered the cost, effectiveness and use of military arms. One effect of this has been to encourage the Japanese to rebuild slowly while the new weapons are being evaluated. Instead of constantly expanding its ground forces—even for 1966 the aim is only 180,000 men—Japan has now begun to put its major effort into small air and sea forces, the 1966 goal being 1,036 airplanes and a military ship tonnage of 143,600. At the same time, it

5

is stressing the modernization of weapons rather than a further expansion of manpower, planning an air force equipped with supersonic Lockheed F-104J Starfighter jets carrying Sidewinder missiles; a sea force built around destroyers, led by the new 3,000-ton Amatsukaze class, to be armed with "Tartar" surface-to-air guided missiles, a modest number of late-type medium-range submarines, and the P2V–7 Neptune patrol plane; as well as a ground air defense which is to include Nike-Ajax missiles, controlled semiautomatically by the BADGE radar warning system.

Thus, by a long and slow process, the Self-Defense Force has been or shortly will be brought to a level at which it could protect the Japanese homeland against attack by any single power in Asia, except the Soviet Union or the United States.

Unquestionably, most Japanese initially accepted the 1952 Security Treaty with the United States with great reluctance as one of the prices of a peace treaty. Since that time, while many continue to wish that the Treaty were not necessary, most have come to prefer it, in its 1960 revised form, to a vastly accelerated rearmament program. They recognize that Japan's major defense depends on it.

Nevertheless, as might be expected, a number of points of friction between Japan and the United States have arisen over the years. The American forces did not move out of the large population centers fast enough after the end of the Occupation to satisfy many Japanese. They were said to create problems of immorality around the bases. They cost the Japanese government money, since it had agreed to share their expenses. They did not release many of the facilities held since the Occupation as fast as the Japanese had anticipated. They retained briefly a special status and thereafter asked for special treatment in Japanese courts. They moved armaments in and out of Japan regardless of popular sensibilities about the "new weapons." They deployed their manpower within Japan and to points outside without advance consultation.

The United States acted frequently to assuage these feelings. In 1954 it negotiated a Mutual Defense Assistance Agreement, under which it granted or leased to Japan nearly all of the major equipment needed for its armed forces. As the years went by, it reduced the share of the American troop costs that Japan was expected to pay, and, as Japan increased its own Self-Defense Force, gradually withdrew its forces, particularly the ground units. But these actions did not satisfy Japan's demands. What the conservative government felt that it had to have was a commitment from the United States stipulating that its troops in Japan would be used primarily for the defense of Japan, a reasonable definition of the Far Eastern area in which the United States might deploy them, a promise that Japan would be consulted on American troop and weapon movements, and the return of the Bonins and Okinawa to Japanese administration. In short, the conservative government, while desiring to retain the benefits of American protection, felt that Japan was, to a certain extent, being used by the United States for American rather than Japanese purposes. These purposes, it was feared, might draw Japan into a war against its own will, and hence its strong desire to eliminate this danger if at all possible. Except for giving up its control of Okinawa and the Bonin Islands, the United States, on her side, was prepared by 1958 to entertain these proposals; and in one form or another they were written into the second Japan-United States Security Pact of 1960.

The new Security Treaty is to run for at least ten years. By its provisions, Japan's fledgling Self-Defense Force will continue to be given the massive umbrella of America's armed might. Both militarily and diplomatically it gives steel to Japan's backbone, enabling Japan to take stronger positions against its potential enemies than it otherwise might.

These rearmament and alliance provisions have necessarily set the framework within which Japan has begun to evolve a new strategic doctrine. From 1945 to 1950, when Japan was totally disarmed, it could plan no defense except reliance on the United States. With the establishment of the National Police Reserve in 1950 it accepted the major responsibility for the maintenance of domestic order and protection against subversion or "indirect aggression." In the debates preceding adoption of the Security Treaty of 1952 it went further to acknowledge its right of self-defense, but preferred to leave "defense" against "external aggression" to the forces of the United States. The American grant of mutual security aid, beginning in 1954, induced it next to accept at least partial responsibility for such defense, at least against direct assault by organized forces in its immediate environs. This, however, is all Japan has accepted to date, except that under the Security Treaty of 1960 the larger area in which it shares a mutual security interest with the United States has been more carefully defined as the "Far East."

Judging from this history and the military strength that Japan aims

7

to have by the end of its present five-year building program in 1966, one may infer that the Japanese government divides the world into three security zones. The primary zone is Japan itself. Here, the government is prepared with its own forces to maintain order and defend itself against external foes; perhaps indefinitely against powers with conventional forces, which today include most of her Asian neighbors, but only for a month or so against total attack by a power with advanced nuclear weapons, such as the Soviet Union, People's China or powers actively supported by them. For prolonged defense against the latter it relies on the deterrent and second-strike power of the United States. This is the major reason why Japan wants the alliance continued. This is also the major reason it has been circumspect in demanding the early return of Okinawa.

The second security zone is the Far East, including South Korea, the Ryukyu and Bonin Islands, Taiwan and their sea and air environs. This is an area within several hundred miles' radius from Japan and therefore, under conditions of limited or conventional warfare, of great strategic significance. Throughout modern times Japan has considered it vital to prevent any part of this region from falling into hostile hands. It was partly to prevent such an eventuality, for example, that Japan fought the Sino-Japanese War of 1894–95 and the Russo-Japanese War of 1904–5. In the postwar period it has been hesitant to revive this doctrine, but by 1958 Premier Kishi felt strong enough to declare that "Japan must do everything it can to prevent Taiwan and Korea from being subjected by the Communists." Public opinion would perhaps not yet support such an extreme view, nor is the government now building forces capable alone of acting on it; and it has no mutual defense understandings with the Korean and Chinese governments in the area. However, under the Japan-United States Security Treaty of 1960, Japanese officials define this Far Eastern zone as the area of mutual Japanese-American security interest and pledge their country to give what facilities the United States might need to defend it.

The rest of the world seems to be conceived of as a tertiary security zone, an area beyond the range of Japan's military influence now and for at least the next five years. Here Japan's primary concern is that the balance of world power shall not shift against its ally, the United States; but the only contribution it feels able to make is gradually to assume greater responsibility closer to home, enabling the United States gradually to concentrate more of its own attention on this outer sphere.

8

Trade and the American Partnership

Throughout modern times the necessity for expanding its trade has occupied a central position in the thinking and planning of the Japanese government. With the land poor in most natural resources, government leaders and even the public at large have been convinced that only through trade can the materials be secured for building a modern industrial society; and only a modern industrial society can provide the standard of living enjoyed by the advanced nations of the West. This conviction underlay Japan's powerful drive for markets in the prewar period, when it utilized its low-paid labor to process textiles and relatively cheap-grade sundries with which it tried, by price competition, to break into the markets, particularly in China, the colonial empires in Southeast Asia, and the United States. For a time it enjoyed remarkable success, but the prospects for the long run were dimmed by the rise of Chinese anti-foreignism, the efforts of the Western powers to limit Japan's access to Southeast Asia, the Great Depression and the protective tariff of the United States. In the end, Japan could not foresee the possibility of securing stable supplies of the resources it felt were necessary for its economic growth and its military strength without bringing the vast reaches of Asia under her direct control. This was at least one of the chains of thinking that dragged Japan down the road to war.

The economic problem is not exactly the same in postwar Japan. Population growth has been brought under control, so that orderly planning is more possible. Improvements in agricultural production have made Japan virtually self-sufficient in foodstuffs. It has now achieved a level of industrial development where it can increasingly compete in quality as well as price, not so much in the light industrial field, which less developed countries are taking over, but in the heavy industrial, electronic and petro-chemical fields, which have hitherto been the province of the advanced nations of the West. Nevertheless, under the leadership of economic administrators-turned-politicians, belief in the importance of foreign trade is even stronger. It is perhaps not too much to say that one of the great lessons that these men learned from their defeat in 1945 was that military strength is hollow without the sustaining power of a healthy economy.

Moreover, their experience with the failure of party government in prewar Japan has taught them that, not only their own continuance in power, but possibly the continuance of the parliamentary system itself, are likewise dependent on the health of the economy. Thus, powerful considerations of both foreign and domestic policy have caused Japan's postwar governments to devote their primary attention to building the economy.

Thanks primarily to their own great efforts and initially to American aid, they have been extraordinarily successful, achieving an annual growth rate of over 9 per cent, probably the highest in the world, and expanding the foreign trade of Japan to a size more than three times greater than before the war. This has been achieved partly by changing the composition of Japan's trade, and partly by changing its direction. No longer does China play a central role. Instead, approximately one-third of its present trade is with South and Southeast Asia, another third with Africa, South America, Canada and Western Europe, and still another third with the United States, which forms the backbone of Japan's new economic structure.

This Japanese-American economic partnership is not without its problems. Both sides have resorted to import restrictions of one kind or another. Since the mid-1950's, American industrialists and labor unions in the cotton textile and cutlery fields, for example, have been protesting that Japanese imports are cutting into the domestic market of American business. They have pressed for relief through tariff increases. The Japanese have tried to prevent such restrictive moves from becoming too damaging to their interests by voluntarily placing quotas on those exports creating most concern, but they do not want these quotas to become permanent or to give what they feel is their legitimate share of the American market to other foreign competitors. Americans, on the other hand, have come to feel that Japan's tariffs and exchange controls have similarly served artificially to limit what they feel should be their share of the Japanese market. Apart from this, U.S.-Japan trade has always suffered from imbalance: the Japanese buy more from us than we do from them. The result has been recurring crises of trade financing, usually tided over by American loans, and a powerful drive by Japan to expand its sales to the United States and to build new markets elsewhere. Nevertheless, these problems have been kept under control, due to the thoughtful attention given them on both sides of the Pacific. Since 1960 a bi-national cabinet-level economic committee has met regularly with the aim of easing the strains in this partnership and placing it on an increasingly strong foundation.

10

Inevitably as stronger economic links have been forged between them, the two countries have become conscious of a growing number of common economic concerns elsewhere. One such concern has been trade policy toward the Communist bloc, in which Japan generally has followed America's lead. Another such concern has been South and Southeast Asia, where it is to the advantage of both countries to promote economic growth and stability. And another is Western Europe, where the formation of the Common Market challenges both countries to find ways to break down its exclusiveness and overcome the greatly increased competitive power of European countries in third markets.

Restraint in Northeast Asia

It is in trying to reestablish a workable relationship with the other countries in the Far Eastern security zone that Japan has faced its most difficult and most sensitive problems. In the north it has been unwilling to reconcile itself to the Soviet occupation of the Habomai and Shikotan Islands off the coast of Hokkaido and the islands of the southern Kuriles; yet, it has been completely frustrated in attempts to recover them by diplomacy. In the west it has been unable to establish a workable relationship with the Republic of Korea.

Japan's relations with Korea have historically been intimate but rarely stable. In modern times Japan has felt that Korea was too close to permit hostile powers to control it and too weak and disunited effectively to control and defend itself. Consequently, beginning late in the nineteenth century the Japanese extended greater and greater influence over the peninsula, finally annexing it in 1910 and ruling it as a colony until 1945. Forced by defeat to give up their control, the Japanese of this generation have moved out of Korea but have continued to watch it closely, even serving perforce as a major base for America's war effort in the Korean war. With the coming into effect of the San Francisco Treaty in 1952, the Japanese government opened negotiations with the new Republic of Korea to establish a relationship on the basis of mutual equality.

True reconciliation, however, has proved to be extraordinarily difficult. Certain real problems have divided the two countries, but perhaps even more divisive has been the atmosphere surrounding these issues, which is charged with the fears, suspicions, hostilities and

11

resentments engendered on both sides by forty years of colonial rule. In addition, the establishment of a normal relationship has been impeded by the abnormal situation that has always obtained in South Korea, where the security of the country depends so largely on the United States. So far negotiations have failed to heal the breach; and Japan has been saved from the necessity of coming firmly to grips with the Korean problem by the continued presence there of the United States.

Japan's relations with the lands in the south and southwestern sectors of the Far Eastern security zone also remain in flux. Close to it are the Bonin and Ryukyu Islands, the latter including the great American military bastion on Okinawa. In the Peace Treaty the United States did not dispute the contention that these islands were indigenous Japanese territory, of which Japan could not rightly be deprived. On the other hand, the United States insisted that it absolutely had to retain these islands as military bases if it was to maintain its position in the western Pacific. The U.S. therefore required Japan to agree in the Treaty that it would approve an American strategic trusteeship over them if one were sought from the United Nations; if one were not sought, then they would remain for the time being under exclusive American administration. Ever since, the United States has firmly insisted that until real peace is restored to the area it will not give up the bases. The Japanese government has made no secret of its desire to recover full control of these islands but, partly perhaps because it recognizes the benefit it derives from the American operation of the bases there and partly no doubt from the recognition of its larger need for a cooperative relationship with the United States, it seems willing not to press its claims to a critical point.

Farther south is the big island of Taiwan, which, like Korea, had long been a Japanese colony. Relations with the Nationalist Chinese government there were established immediately after the San Francisco Conference, and trade has been fostered; but there are few Japanese, either in the government or out, who expect this to be more than a temporary arrangement.

It is perhaps fair to say that in this zone of greatest importance to Japanese security Japan is potentially revisionist, which means that Japan is not satisfied to maintain the status quo indefinitely. On the other hand, the position that the new Japan ultimately will seek in northeast Asia is not yet clear, for it has not yet made its bid.

So far it has preferred to accept the United States as the stabilizing force there, while it concentrates its own energies on rebuilding itself.

The Return to Southeast Asia

Since hunger for the resources of Southeast Asia and the dream of hegemony over that region had largely animated Japan's urge to war, it was widely feared by the people of these lands that, when Japan received its independence, it would return aggressively and try to seize the same prizes by other means. The United States' concern was different. It did not fear Japan's return; rather it welcomed it, confident that Japan would not revive its imperialist policies and hopeful that it would help to provide capital, goods, leadership and eventually perhaps even protection to the new states that appeared so inviting to Communist infiltration. Contrary to both expectations, Japan's return to Southeast Asia has been slow and cautious.

For most of the postwar period Japan has been troubled by reparations problems. In the San Francisco Treaty Japan had accepted the obligation to compensate in some measure those countries it had overrun during the war, but the amounts remained to be negotiated. The United States had written into the Peace Treaty that payments should not be exacted to the extent of jeopardizing Japan's own economic recovery; and the Japanese characteristically talked a poor mouth. On the other hand, the receiving powers were all new states, desperately in need of external support if they were to get their economies moving. They were impressed by the high level of Japan's development and its rapid postwar recovery. Except for the Nationalist Chinese government on Taiwan, which for political reasons decided to forego its rights to reparations, they were in no mood to accept Japan's very limited estimates of its ability to pay. The negotiations, therefore, were long drawn out. The first reparations agreement, a provisional one with Burma, was not signed until September 1954. The Philippines signed next, in 1956, Indonesia in 1958, and South Vietnam in 1959. The Thailand special yen account was not settled until 1962, and Burmese reparations were not finally agreed on until 1963. Japan has thus obligated itself to pay $1.018 billion to these countries; by the end of 1963 it was at about the halfway mark in its payments.

In the beginning the Japanese government looked on these payments simply as a penalty. As time went on, however, it came to see that they might be made to serve as an important part of a general campaign to rebuild its economic relations with these countries. It is in that light that they are now primarily seen, since they provide for payments in goods and loans which, in turn, are playing an important part in opening up new sources of supply and new markets. At the same time, in recent years, the government has been adding to them a modest public and private investment program (about $120 million was privately invested from 1950 to 1963), a program of leader exchanges, and a program of technological assistance. By the end of 1960 more than 2,600 Asians had been accepted for technical training in Japan, and 300 Japanese specialists had been sent to assist Asian countries. Four technical training centers had been established overseas. From 1954 to 1963 Japanese trade with South and Southeast Asia had more than doubled.

This advancing economic policy has been coupled with a political policy of reconciliation. Deeply conscious of its Asian history and culture, Japan has tried to appeal to the nations of this region as an Asian among Asians. It attended the Bandung Conferences, has been active in ECAFE, and has striven for acceptance and leadership within the Afro-Asian bloc in the United Nations.

To a certain extent Japan's diplomacy of persuasion has mollified its southern neighbors. They are growing more eager for Japanese capital, Japanese goods, Japanese know-how and Japanese diplomatic support. But the success has been limited. Great as the regional trade expansion has been, the rate of increase is actually less than for Japan's over-all trade. In fact, whereas 1954 exports to these countries of South and Southeast Asia represented 28 per cent of Japan's total exports, in 1963 their share had fallen off to 18 per cent and the share of Japan's total imports represented by imports from these countries had fallen from 19 per cent in 1954 to 14 per cent in 1963. Compared with the prewar situation in 1938, when Japanese trade with Southeast Asia accounted for 38 per cent of its total imports and 60 per cent of its total exports, the decline of the arc of Asia in Japan's trade is even more dramatic. In short, while Japan is today the greatest economic power in Asia, it is less related economically to Asia than at any time in its recent history.

This has been a disappointment to many Japanese. Two explanations have impressed Japanese economists. One is political. A number of these new Asian states have been so unsettled and so unused to the problem of building stable international relations that sustained negotiations have frequently been impossible. In addition, the fear of colonialism and the preoccupation with nationalism are so strong in these countries that their governments have been extremely reluctant to pass the laws and create the political environment necessary to attract Japanese investors and traders. The second explanation is economic. Their economies being in the early stages of development, these countries in most cases still depend heavily on one or two main agricultural products as their main export items. Japan, in turn, no longer needs such large volumes of these products as, for example, rice, and in many cases it can secure those it does need as, for example, cotton, from the United States or elsewhere. In the light industrial field, many of these countries are now developing their own production, so that they not only are not so dependent on imports from Japan as in prewar days, but threaten to compete. And in the chemical and heavy industrial field, which is accounting for an increasing share of regional imports, Japanese exporters are meeting serious competition from Western Europe and the United States.

In part these problems are indigenous to the region, but in part they are also common to relations between other advanced and underdeveloped economies. Contrary to the assumptions that prevailed in the age of imperialism, it now appears that the trade which can develop between these types of economies is less than that which develops among the most highly advanced economies. The answer then would appear to lie in Japan's promoting the development of its neighbors in Asia as rapidly as possible. This it is determined to do, but obviously this will take a long time, and Japan alone does not have the enormous quantity of capital or technical skill that will be needed. Moreover, if economic development is to accord with a rational division of labor within the region, the cooperation not only of Japan but of all the nations of the region and many outside it will be needed.

On Guard Against Communist China and the Soviet Union

The American alliance, military, economic and cultural, has drawn Japan into the vast network of ties that the United States has organized against the Communist powers. Japan has been careful to cooperate faithfully with the diplomatic and other measures advocated by the United States, including, for example, refraining from recognizing the new Communist powers, applying restrictions to its trade with them in strategic goods, and refraining from trade agreements that might be expected to expand commercial relations beyond a minimal level. Unlike many of America's allies, it has even recognized the Chinese government on Taiwan. Moreover, to parallel American policy, it has dealt with the Communist powers differentially, as for instance in 1956, by restoring state relations with the Soviet Union but not with the Communist governments of mainland China or North Korea.

The decision to boycott the Chinese Communist regime on the mainland politically was taken by the Yoshida government in the months preceding the San Franciso Conference as one of the prices it felt it had to pay to secure an end to the Occupation, even though it was clear that not all contacts with the mainland Chinese could be avoided. Negotiations between non-governmental bodies were soon instituted in order to secure the repatriation of the many Japanese then being detained on Chinese territory, to stabilize conditions for Japanese fisheries in the East China Sea, to facilitate limited trade and to organize exchanges of delegations from various economic, social and cultural bodies. The Chinese government, in turn, has regularly sought to use these relations as instruments of its so-called "people's diplomacy." It has steadily sought to persuade the Japanese people to pressure their government into altering its basic foreign policy posture. What the Chinese want is for Japan to renounce the Security Treaty with the United States, withdraw recognition from the government on Taiwan, recognize Peking and take the road to socialism and neutralism.

Sometimes the Chinese work primarily through the Japan Communist Party. In recent years, they have repeatedly expressed their growing satisfaction with and confidence in the JCP leadership and line. At other times, however, they have seemed more inclined to work through the Japan Socialist Party, being impressed by its loyalty to socialism and neutralism and by its strength as Japan's second largest political party. China's sudden decision to cut off trade in the spring of 1958, for example, has been seen by many to have been a forceful, if unsuccessful, attempt to embarrass the conservatives and to boost the Socialists in the general election of that year. On the other hand, there are times when the Chinese seem to despair of the success of revolution in Japan, whether Communist, Socialist, or led by a united front, and turn instead to wooing the sympathetic, China-trade-minded leaders of big business and the ruling Liberal-Democratic Party.

These offensives have had a number of receptive Japanese attitudes to play upon. Cultural relations between these two countries have been so profound over the past 2,000 years that many Japanese continue to respond sympathetically to the old phrase *dôbun dôshu*, which means that they and the Chinese are one in script and one in race. Other Japanese are drawn by the same dream that for so long agitated American traders: the dream of the China market. In spite of the fact that Japan has more than recovered its prewar international economic position without benefit of the China trade, many Japanese remain convinced that a great trade awaits them in China if only political obstacles can be overcome. Others are drawn to China by feelings of guilt for Japanese conduct in China during the war.

Whether or not mainland China will be able to persuade the Japanese to change their present attitudes in the years ahead will depend on the relative balance of power in the region. In the military field China's nuclear tests and refusal to sign the partial test-ban treaty are matters of great concern to Japan; but so far the Chinese have not developed the navy, the air force or the missile delivery systems that would force the Japanese to consider them a serious military threat. Nevertheless Japan, which now arms almost exclusively against the Soviet Union, may soon face a choice between greater armaments and more reliance on the United States or increasing concessions to China. In addition, should the Communist Chinese gain in economic strength, they might well be able to step up their pressure on Japan by resorting to trade war, particularly in Southeast Asia.

On the other hand, given China's growing split with the Soviet Union and the continued growth of Japan's strength, the military and economic balance of power in future years seems likely to shift even more heavily in Japan's favor. If, therefore, present trends continue, the pressures for concession on Japan may be expected to weaken, and it may well be China that will be faced with the dilemma of considering a change of course.

Japan's attitude and policy toward the Soviet Union is similarly guarded, but largely for different reasons. The Japanese are united to the Soviets by no bonds of traditional culture or memory of prewar trade. They feel no guilt for the war. Quite the contrary, they feel that it was the Soviet Union which betrayed them, attacking Japan when the war was nearly over and then demanding territorial concessions (southern Sakhalin and the Kuriles) that nearly all Japanese feel are unjust and disproportionate. On the other hand, in 1956 Japan did negotiate a peace declaration with the U.S.S.R. and has resumed normal trade and other relations. The reasons for these developments are that the Soviet Union gave up its joint insistence with the Chinese that Japan should change her fundamental international posture; that the United States—at least since 1955—did not seek to prevent it; and that Japan was influenced by fear of prolonging the antagonism in the face of overwhelming Soviet power, a fear that otherwise it could not recover its fishery position in the northwestern Pacific, and a hope that a political *rapprochement* might lead to expanded trade, particularly in view of the U.S.S.R.'s development plans for Siberia. Thus, Japan's attitude toward the Soviet Union essentially remains one of mistrust and fear, but flavored with hope, while toward mainland China it is one of self-confidence and sympathy, tinged with apprehension.

How stable is this policy of cautious alignment? This depends in part on the continuity of the international forces to which it has been shaped as a response, the inability of Japan to go it alone, the strength of the United States vis-à-vis the Soviet Union in northeast Asia, the hardness of the Communist Chinese line and the softness of its military means, and the ability of the United States and the rest of the non-Communist world to help Japan meet its major needs for security, economic growth and cultural enrichment. It depends also on the continuity in power of the shapers of this policy: Japan's conservative party.

II. CONTROL AT HOME

The Strength of the Conservatives

The foreign policy of alignment with America is the program of the "conservatives." It is their constant victory at the polls that has made it the policy of the country. Since the San Francisco Treaty (and even before) the "conservatives" have won every election to the House of Representatives, giving them a control ranging from 70 per cent of the seats following the general election of 1952 to 61 per cent following that of 1963. Their control in the second house, or House of Councillors, has been less marked but has risen from a low of 54 per cent of the seats after the 1953 election to a high of 57 per cent after the election in July 1963. This control of the Diet by the "conservatives" has also enabled them to retain continuous control of the Cabinet.

Their strength may be partly explained by the skill of the "conservatives" and their parties in the political arts. Deriving organizationally and in many ways ideologically from the majority parliamentary parties of the prewar period, they have been able to exploit certain traditional voting habits. They have also shown themselves more highly skilled in the techniques of party organization than their competitors. Out of the welter of postwar parties they managed by 1955 to form a single Liberal-Democratic Party embracing all "conservatives"; and particularly since 1959 they have been making strenuous efforts to expand their membership and build effective local organizations and affiliates. Thus, the Liberal-Democrats are today the largest and most effectively organized party in Japan.

Annual reports issued by the government as well as the reports of newsmen also testify to the superior ability of the "conservatives" in getting financial contributions.

More experienced, better organized and better financed, the "conservatives" are also better led. They have been better able to attract into their ranks many of the leaders of the "establishment," both locally and nationally; and this has given them a distinct advantage in electoral appeal and in formulating realistic policy. It is difficult, of course, to be sure what exactly influences the voter, the party organizer or the campaign contributor to support one party or another, whether, for example, it is primarily issues or personalities, and, if issues, which ones in particular. But it seems reasonable to believe that the two major platforms of the "conservatives"—economic growth and alignment with the United States—have won for them a solid measure of mass support. In the matter of foreign policy, national public opinion polls have shown, for instance, that at least one-third and possibly closer to one-half of the Japanese people have come to favor the alliance policy. Lastly, the "conservatives" enjoy the fruits of past victory since, by holding office, they are able to enjoy the prestige and dispense the influence that helps win elections in the future.

The "conservatives" are often spoken of as the party of business. This is largely because many of the Diet members of the Liberal-Democratic Party have direct personal connections with business. Moreover, they derive their financial support largely from business federations and from individual firms; and their policies have accorded broadly with the business point of view. On the other hand, they win electoral support from the farmers and the middle-income groups in the cities. They have been particularly able in establishing close relations not only with the big business federations like *Keidanren* and *Nikkeiren* but also with farmers' groups like the Agricultural Cooperative Associations and with special-interest groups like the veterans, repatriates and workers in personal service occupations. They are in fact broadly based in nearly every sector of the population and throughout the country.

So impressive has been the Liberal-Democratic Party's hold that increasing concern is expressed on the Japanese Left that the "conservatives" may have found the ballot tree, enabling them to build a "permanent majority." Unafraid of the opposition, confident of victory in the next election, they may and, the Leftists charge, often do, run roughshod over the views of the minority, perverting their dominant position into a "tyranny of the majority."

Americans, used to the ways of moderation and compromise, and reassured by the attractiveness of the "conservatives'" foreign policy, have been inclined to assume that conservatism is generally the same the world over. A few years ago Hirotatsu Fujiwara, a Meiji University professor and prominent political commentator, visited seven factional heads of the Liberal-Democratic Party and discussed with them their conceptions of life, society and politics.* His findings are interesting to compare with Clinton Rossiter's recent study of conservatism in America.† Conservatives in both countries are primarily men of the "establishment." They share a preference for order, aristocracy, property, religious and patriotic tradition, and pragmatic methods. Neither group comprises philosophers. Both are inclined to talk as though man's salvation is a moral problem, but characteristically to act as though it were essentially an economic one. All of this has made them both anti-Communist. With the growth of the conservative persuasion in postwar America, this congeniality of temperament has helped the two nations to work together more closely than ever before.

On the other hand, the differences in the two conservatisms is equally important. For one thing, the traditional values that have given stability to Japan are quite different from those in America. The former stress the subordination of the individual to the group, whether it is one's family, one's co-workers and employer, or one's nation. The latter asserts the pre-eminence of the individual and his rights. The faith of one is rooted in an ideal of Confucian harmony, the faith of the other in a tradition of Christian personality in a pluralistic society. These differences of faith are reinforced by differences in the composition and historical experience of the "establishment" in the two countries. In Japan it has traditionally been the bureaucracy, whether military, civilian or both, that exercised preponderant power. Other political as well as economic and religious forces have been relatively weak. Accordingly there has developed a habit of dependence on government quite at odds with Western traditions in which business and, in some cases, church and party express their independence and even suspicion of government. Nor

* Hirotatsu Fujiwara, "Jiyū-Minshutō no Seiji Kankaku," *Chūō Kōron,* February 1959, pp. 58-84.

† Clinton L. Rossiter, *Conservatism in America* (2nd rev. ed.; New York: Vintage, 1962).

should another very obvious difference be forgotten: the patriotism of each is directed toward different lands. Japanese conservatives are concerned about the recovery of Okinawa, for example, as American conservatives would be for the recovery of Hawaii if that island group were seized by Japan.

Moreover, conservatism in Japan is less moderate than in America. With the temporary collapse of the traditional order after the defeat of 1945 and the subsequent emergence of rapidly changing and competing forces in Japanese society, the footing for conservatives became unsure, with the result that they are now inclined less to "standpattism," to use Rossiter's phrase, than to reaction. True, they are bent on stabilizing the institutions of property, morality and patriotism, but these institutions have been so badly shaken that they find themselves often faced with the need to restore what they can of the faith and society that was, rather than to maintain the situation that is. The durable leader Bamboku Ono (who died in the spring of 1964) is quoted by Fujiwara as saying how revolted he was at the sight of the demonstrations at the time of the Oji Paper Company strike. Red flags were raised, he recalled, "like the Heike at Dan-no-ura."* He saw revolution all about him and felt that Japan was being occupied by the Red Army. But, even as he spoke, a contrasting vision came before his eyes. He saw long lines of country people, stretched for miles along a dusty road, waiting to catch a glimpse of the Emperor as he passed by. When the Emperor's entourage approached, they raised their voices in a mighty shout, "Banzai! Banzai!" until the heavens shook. "*They,*" said Ono, "are real Japanese." Needless to say, this was a memory out of the past, but it perhaps reveals some of the feeling that underlies the conservative proposals for promulgating a public code of ethics, enlarging the duties of the police, restricting demonstrations in the vicinity of the Diet, or revising the constitutional status of the Emperor—all of which proposals would require, not just preservation of the status quo, but a policy of bold reaction.

Finally, there is another common characteristic of Japanese and American conservatives that shapes them differently: their pragmatism. As just noted, the Japanese leaders are more inclined do-

* Toward the end of the twelfth century Japan was convulsed by an epic struggle for control of the country between two rival military clans, the Heike, who bore red standards, and the Genji, who bore white standards. The climax came at Dan-no-ura, where in 1185 the last of the Heike were driven into the sea.

22

mestically to force issues than are the Americans; internationally, however, their inclinations are reversed. Perhaps this is because amid opposing forces at home they feel strong, whereas amid the cold war in the world arena they feel weak. Be that as it may, the conservative leaders who most strongly support the American alliance, for example, do so partly on the ideological grounds of anti-Communism but even more on the pragmatic grounds of Japanese nationalism. Japan's weakness makes it necessary for survival to associate with the strong. This penchant for allying with what is perceived at the time to be the strongest power in the world, at one time Britain, later Germany, now the United States, is one of Japan's strongest diplomatic traditions. Dissimilar as this is from America's own isolationist past, it today draws the two countries together; but the important point is that this conservative policy of alignment with America depends primarily on the pragmatic tests of military power and trade advantages rather than on a supposed common allegiance to "free world" values.

In short, while it is not entirely apt, the relationship between American and Japanese conservatives may be described in part by the old Japanese phrase: lying in the same bed but dreaming different dreams.

This same phrase may also describe the relationship among the Japanese conservative leaders themselves. Formed by a merger of two parties in 1954, the conservative grouping is not so much a unified organization or even a wedding of two organizations as it is a coalition of factions, each made up of Diet members who give their loyal support to certain leading figures. Due largely to the traditional style of Japanese leadership and the parliamentary system of election to the premiership, these figures are generally "organization men": intelligent, educated, technically skilled and effective in intimate group relations. Each owes his position in the party and government largely to the strength of a personal organization that he has managed over the years to hold together by force of personality, favorable social connections, the funds he can attract and dispense, and the office or influence he can pass along.

As leader types they have no close counterparts in American politics. They act in some of the style of American Senators but in the end rarely break party discipline. Moreover, they are fewer than Senators in number and their individual influence is far greater. Each has a national organization that is, in effect, the nucleus of a potential national party. Each is a publicly identified candidate for the premiership and therefore a rival of the Prime Minister. On the other hand, none is strong enough to become Prime Minister on his own, and none can call on widespread support from the electorate. In fact, if we believe the public opinion polls, rarely has even a Prime Minister been given the accolade of national popularity by the voters. Ultimate victory then depends on the individual's skill in holding his faction together and in inter-factional maneuvering in the never-ending effort to build, maintain or destroy a majority coalition within the Party.

The Socialists are fond of saying that the intra-party struggle among the "conservatives" is really a game of musical chairs: that these men are so much alike and pass into and out of Cabinets so often that it makes little difference which one is Prime Minister at any particular time. It is true, as we have shown, that they do share a certain broad outlook on life and politics, and it is also true that they therefore compromise with each other, making violent shifts in policy very unlikely. On the other hand, each does have his own style, and certain of them have been identified with characteristic policy positions.

The foreign policy of alignment with America, for example, has been championed largely by those factions led by leaders of the so-called "Yoshida school." Shigeru Yoshida, who was Prime Minister when this foreign policy first evolved, retired from active factional leadership when his Cabinet fell in the fall of 1954, but he re-emerged a few years later in the role of elder statesman, exerting his influence to bring to power men of his choosing and to preserve intact the policy of alignment. It has been the heads of these "alignment factions" who have secured the highest leadership in Yoshida's wake: Nobusuke Kishi, from 1957 to 1960, Hayato Ikeda, from 1960 to 1964, and Eisako Sato, from 1964 to the present. Each, like Yoshida, is a national university graduate, with long experience in the prewar and wartime bureaucracy. Three other faction leaders who are more independent of the Yoshida influence may also be identified as part of the alignment wing in foreign policy. They are the elderly Mitsujirō Ishii, a man with experience in prewar governmental administration, the newspaper world, and the Seiyūkai party; and Aiichirō Fijiyama, the businessman-turned-politician who, as Kishi's Foreign Minister, led the fight for the revised Security Pact. The two successors to the Kishi mantle, Shōjirō Kawashima and Takeo Fukuda, also supporters of this policy.

There are, however, other conservative leaders of a different type with a different approach to foreign policy. Like Ishii and Kawashima, they are primarily graduates of private universities, chiefly Waseda and Meiji, who have had long experience in business, newspaper work and particularly in party politics. Often referred to as "pure politicians," they include the late Ichirō Kōno, whose concerns were chiefly agriculture, fisheries and better relations with the U.S.S.R.; Kenzō Matsumura, a man of long experience in prewar politics, a leader in the "left conservative" Progressive and Democratic Parties after the war, and a minister in the second Hatoyama Cabinet; Takeo Miki, the youngest of the top faction leaders, a close collaborator of Matsumura's and like him a graduate of the Progressive Party and then the "Hatoyama school"; and Tanzan Ishibashi, Japan's leading economic publicist and ex-Prime Minister, whose special concern today is to improve relations with mainland China. These factions do not form a permanent bloc in the Party. Their leaders sometimes participate in Cabinets with factional leaders of the alignment wing and sometimes do not. But they do share an inclination toward a foreign policy different from that which has prevailed.

Their preference is for a foreign policy of armed, independent regionalism. They would have Japan pull away from its exclusively American orientation. In fact, their reservations about the revised Security Pact were one of the chief reasons why the Liberal-Democratic Party required two years to formulate a clear and concrete policy on the revision, the final price of even limited cooperation having been Kishi's retirement. They would draw closer to mainland China and the Soviet Union in an effort to strengthen Japan's regional position in East Asia, but they would not do so from a posture of weakness. Since they prefer not to rely as heavily on the American alliance, they would probably be drawn into a policy of stepped-up rearmament. It will be recalled that Hatoyama, who was associated with these Party elements, was one of the first to call for rearmament. These groups, which may be characterized by virtue of their views on foreign policy as "independence factions," succeeded in capturing the prime ministership briefly with Ichirō Hatoyama from 1954 to 1956, when relations with the U.S.S.R. were restored, and for a few months in the winter of 1956-57, with Tanzan Ishibashi. Since then they have been eclipsed.

In the outcome, the American alignment policy has depended on the continued successes of the Liberal-Democratic Party at the polls and on that of the "alignment factions" within that Party. A corollary to this has been the dependence of that policy on the weakness of the "independence factions" within the Party and of the "progressives" outside the Party.

The Weakness of the "Progressives"

All Japanese parties of the Left are customarily referred to as "progressive," which means that they seek fundamental changes in Japanese culture, society and policy to bring it more into accord with what they feel are the healthy forces of modern life. Some Japanese "progressives," particularly on the Socialist Right, think of themselves as the Japanese counterparts of Western liberals. The similarities are there. Contemporary American liberals and Japanese "progressives" are temperamentally akin in placing a high value on reason and theory, individual rights, social and economic equality, and the "people," particularly the underprivileged. These and other similarities help explain why so many Japanese "progressive intellectuals" felt so let down when most liberal American intellectuals criticized their attitudes and actions at the time of the Security Pact demonstrations in 1960.

But the two societies have undergone different experiences with the result that this temperament in America has come to occupy a middle ground, confident of the good will of all classes, trusting that, with vigilance, the government is the agent of the "people," and believing therefore in orderly political action through elected representatives. This pattern has been broken only under the most severe provocation as in the case of the current desegregation campaigns, in which some liberals have participated in orderly civil disobedience. In Japan, the long experience with oligarchic rule, the hardships that are the inevitable accompaniment of rapid modernization, and the greater isolation from the rest of the world— in short, longer and more severe provocation—has often bent this temperament either into a restless conservatism or, usually, into "progressivism," where, particularly on the Socialist Left, it has, in varying degrees, accepted the concepts of class struggle, the hostility of the government to the "people," the need for mass mobilization, and the inevitability of revolution or at least fundamental change.

It is this unique syndrome of liberal and socialist elements that draws the "progressives" into a community of feeling separating them from the "conservatives." It also has given rise to certain broad approaches to foreign policy, which might be described as disarmed, neutral regionalism. Today Communists and Socialists alike call for an abrupt turn away from the American alignment, a reversal of the rearmament trend, a move toward establishing as good relations as possible with the Communist bloc, and reliance on neutrality.

Having said this, we have probably gone too far, for within the "progressive" movement there is little unity, and much argument on all of these points. The movement is currently split into three parties: the Communist, the Socialist and the Democratic-Socialist. Of these, it is the Socialist Party that is the most significant, the other two having relatively little voter appeal. And the Socialist Party itself is not a well-coordinated organization but a coalition, led largely by Diet members, labor leaders and intellectuals who today are loyal to one or another of the factional heads. These heads include, on the Left, Kōzō Suzuki, leader of the more radical, pro-Chinese element of the former Suzuki faction and Chairman of the party since May 1965; Masaru Nomizo, who like Sasaki came up through the farmers' movement; and Hisao Kuroda, especially active in the peace and farmers' movements, whose position is so extreme that he has spent most of the postwar years outside the Socialist Party, heading his own Labor-Farmer Party. Opposed to these men today are the Right-wing and moderate leaders, including Jōtarō Kawakami, former Chairman of the party and long-time leader of the moderates who remain within it; Saburō Eda, champion of pragmatic socialism, who split with Suzuki to win for himself and then to pass on to his associate, Tomomi Narita, the strategic secretary-generalship of the party today; and Hiroo Wada, an ex-governmental agricultural official, who switched from the Left to support Narita.

Socialists—and Communists as well—are fond of explaining that the factional disputes within their parties are the result of ideological and policy differences whereas those in the "conservative" ranks stem from petty questions of personal relations having no significance for policy. We have already seen that this is an oversimplified view of the "conservatives." As for the "progressives," it is true that at certain times the various factions do take rather clear positions according to their individual lights, from the Fabian socialism of some of the Kawakami group to the Marxism-Leninism of the Kuroda group. On the other hand, the relative weakness of each of the factions makes intra-party alliance as necessary for control in the Socialist Party as in the Liberal-Democratic Party. In both parties one often finds strange bedfellows.

These personal rivalries and ideological and policy differences within the "progressive" camp have been a serious handicap. There are others as well. Unlike the "conservatives," the "progressives" have no long prewar history of mass support to build on. They are small in membership and poorly organized locally. In fact, most localities have no Socialist or Democratic-Socialist Party organization at all; and they have extremely meager representation in local and prefectural assemblies. Having never come to power in the national government, except in the coalition cabinets of 1947 and 1948, they are weak in the prestige and authority that officeholding gives. Although a number of their intellectual advisers are social theorists of distinction, the "progressive parties" are weak in the knowledge and experience vital to practical policy-making. Excluding the Communists perhaps, they are in large part dependent on the big labor federations for organization and money, and almost as heavily for leaders, candidates and ideas.

These and other difficulties have not prevented them from expanding their influence. As a matter of fact, if one groups the various "progressive" parties together, they have increased their voter support from 22 per cent in the general election of 1946 to 40 per cent in the general election of 1963, and at one time in 1947-48—a time of great political instability to be sure—they even managed to participate in coalition governments under Katayama and then Ashida. Yet, generally speaking, their role so far has been largely negative. Under extreme provocation they have been able to marshal sufficient mass support, for example, to cause the "conservatives" to withdraw the Police Duties Revision bill in 1958 and even to bring down the Kishi cabinet in 1960. But they have not been able to force the "conservatives" to accept their own "progressive" programs and have not been able to attain power.

The Failure of the Middle

One of the symbols most often used by Japan's politicians to portray the role they feel Japan is destined to play in the world is that of the bridge: Japan as the bridge between East and West, the integrator of the Asian and Occidental cultures, the healer of mankind's cold war disease. The symbol stems partly from their dreams of peace and leadership. It also stems from one of their deepest-felt needs at home, the need to build bridges among the many isolated, communal, in many ways familistic, groups that make up Japanese society, and in the postwar period, particularly between the "conservatives" and the "progressives." But the bridges have failed. For the past seventeen years Japanese society has been divided at home almost as seriously as the world is divided abroad.

In the first confusing years following surrender, parties were formed at nearly every point in the political spectrum. Both the prewar conservative and progressive movements had moderate wings that found themselves side by side. There were the conservative party politicians, particularly from the Minseitō party, like Bukichi Miki and Ichirō Kōno and a few ex-officials like Hitoshi Ashida, who made up the core of the new Progressive (later Democratic) Party, and called for progress toward a "reformed capitalism." Another group was formed by the Fabian, Christian and other moderate socialists, particularly men of long experience in the prewar trade union movement like Tetsu Katayama and Suehiro Nishio, who sought an orderly, peaceful transition to socialism by democratic processes. These men joined the reorganized Japan Socialist Party, forming a Right-wing bloc within it. In addition there was the Co-operative Party, led by men primarily dedicated to the cooperative movement in rural society. Together these centrist groups polled nearly a third of the Japanese electorate in the early postwar years. Their common moderation, pragmatism and devotion to democratic processes would seem to have provided the possibility of organizing a powerful centrist party or parties. Indeed, the necessities of multi-party politics did bring them together into a working coalition in the Katayama and Ashida cabinets of 1947 and 1948. But, after this high point, the attraction of moderation weakened and the pull to Right and Left grew, with the result that in 1955 Right-wing Socialists turned their backs on the Democrats to join the Socialist Left; and the Democrats in turn threw in their lot with the more conservative bureaucratic forces of the Liberal Party.

The event was hailed at the time as the birth of a two-party system. In a sense it was. From that time on there have been only two important parties in Japanese politics: the Liberal-Democratic and the Socialist. On the other hand, they have not provided the vehicle for keeping government close and responsive to the people either by respect for each other's views or by alternation in office. Rather, the two-party formulation of 1955 has wiped out the moderate movements as a promising center of political organization and leadership and drawn them into compromise, not with each other, but with the more extreme forms of progressivism and conservatism respectively. The bridges were burned and the two major political leaderships in Japan thereafter have stood confronting each other from opposite sides of a deep divide, calling to the people below to give up the ways of moderation and conciliation and take up stations on one side of the valley or the other, ready either to demonstrate in the streets under the Socialists' red banners or to back up the police behind the barricades.

In the fall of 1959 a new effort was made by some of the Right-wing Socialists, led particularly by Suehiro Nishio, to break away from the extremists and plant a standard on the middle ground. The Democratic-Socialist Party was formed. As one of its leaders, House of Councillors member Eki Sone, explained, they hope to attract workers, farmers and small businessmen with a program of respect for the processes of parliamentary democracy in political affairs, a moderate socialism of the mixed-economy type in economic affairs, and a gradual pulling away from the American alignment toward a true neutralism in foreign affairs. They find their models in the pragmatic, democratic socialists of Britain and Western Europe. But they have made no headway. They have failed at the polls, their numbers in the House of Representatives declining from 40 when they formed their party to 17 following the November 1960 election and rising only to 23 following the election of 1963. Yet even this slight increase in seats in 1963 is misleading, since popular electoral support actually continued to decline, from 8.87 per cent in 1960 to 7.27 per cent in 1963.

Why should this be, and is this situation likely to continue? In the immediate instance of the Democratic-Socialists, they suffer from many of the same weaknesses as the Socialists, only in more extreme form: they lack money, attractive candidates and effective organization. Like the Socialist Party, they are dependent in large part on a friendly supporting labor organization, the *Dōmei Kaigi*, which cannot compete numerically with *Sōhyō* in the labor field and certainly not with organized business in the national economic arena.

Deeper and more fundamental than these reasons may be the lack of consensus in postwar Japanese society. During the past hundred years the Japanese people have been uprooted from their traditional way of life, pulled through a modern revolution, subjected to war, defeat and occupation, and now thrust into a divided world. Small wonder that they have not reacted uniformly to these events. In fact, their response has been so various, depending on variables such as age, social position, occupation, education and locality, that in the postwar period the very core of Japanese nationalism itself has been shaken. In short, while there are groups taking a middle position on various issues and there are those who believe in moderation and cooperation, their specific views and their organizational ties are disparate. They have been unable to find a common ground of assumptions about man, society, political goals and political behavior, that is, a common ground of Japanese nationality. It may be supposed therefore that moderate parties of the center are unlikely to replace or even seriously to compete with the "progressives" and the "conservatives" until the pace of change has slowed and the Japanese people have sufficient time in peace and prosperity to regain confidence in each other.

Another underlying explanation for this weakness of the center seems to be sociological. In spite of the century-long process of modernization and the postwar economic expansion, a large, coherent middle class has not yet developed. The components would appear to be there in the so-called "old middle class" of white-collar salaried people, and even workers are now said to be undergoing incorporation into the middle class. But there is little spontaneous recognition by these elements of common interests. The facts are that the medium and small business entrepreneurs, their families and employees are among the most economically insecure elements in Japanese society, in contrast to the farmers, who are today rather well off. On the other hand, both of these elements are traditionally conservative, the agents of higher authority in the institutions of Japanese social control. In this, they are at odds with the "new middle class," which is on an economic level akin to organized labor and finds its most congenial attitude to be one of social protest.

Thus, the three main elements of the Japanese middle class have found it impossible to get together. Each has gone its own way organizationally. The farmers have organized a number of farmers' associations that generally play the role of pressure groups, either affiliating openly with the conservative party or at least finding it

31

expedient to work with it. The white-collar employee has generally followed the path of unionization and affiliation, via *Sōhyō* or *Dōmei* with the socialist parties.

Last to organize have been the medium and small enterprise groups; and, since they employ about one-half of the industrial labor force, observers in recent years have felt that a powerful new support organization might be built out of them. In 1956 a particularly vigorous movement was launched by the ex-Nissan magnate, Gisuke Ayukawa, to organize this sector into the new *Chuseiren* Political Federation of Medium and Small Enterprise; but, after an impressive beginning, the movement became rather thoroughly discredited in 1959 when Ayukawa's son was found guilty of violating the election laws in his bid for the House of Councillors. Since then the influence of the *Chuseiren* has declined, and the small businessmen of Japan, their families and their employees remain divided organizationally and ineffective politically.

The Trend Toward an Independent Foreign Policy

How long will this configuration of Japanese politics continue? Japan has undergone such fundamental changes in recent years and its political currents intermingle so complexly that one cannot predict with certainty which of the contradictory currents will dominate the main stream and which will be pushed aside to dissipate themselves in quiet eddies.

Although the conservatives continue to be strong at the polls, their popularity has been steadily declining. If this trend continues unabated, it is possible that sometime within the next decade the progressive parties may together command a majority and attempt to displace conservative rule. This is by no means certain, however, for it would seem to require the progressives to unite or at least form a working coalition. The history of the movement and its present divisions suggest that this may be difficult indeed. In fact, for the past several years the trend within Japanese progressivism has been not toward unification but toward increasingly severe confrontations between the moderates and the extremists. At the Left of the progressive spectrum the Communist Party shows no signs of giving up its independent position, nor have the other progressive parties shown any signs of accepting it in a united front. Hence there is every indication that the JCP will continue to go its own way.

In 1961 the party attempted to solidify its leadership and its ideological position by purging the dissidents and adopting a new program. It has also strengthened its youth work by taking the lead in organizing a new front organization, the *Minseidō* or Democratic Youth League, which has now built a membership of between 80,000 and 100,000. Moreover, it has greatly expanded the circulation of its publications. In elections for the House of Councillors it boosted its popular vote between 1959 and 1962 from 1.9 per cent to 3.1 per cent in the national constituency and from 3.3 per cent to 4.8 per cent in the prefectural constituencies. In the general election for the House of Representatives it won 2.9 per cent of the total vote in 1960 and 4.7 per cent in 1963.

This does not, however, reflect an alarming rate of growth. Moreover, the Communists still continue to suffer from divided leadership. In fact, the tendency toward Party splits seems to be endemic since Japanese intellectuals find Party discipline uncongenial. Recently the rivalry of the Chinese and the Russians divided the leadership into "Chinese" and "Russian" factions. After a series of splits and purges, the "Chinese" faction has consolidated control, causing many disillusioned Communists to leave the party. These defectors have taken up positions very similar to those of the Socialist Party. They usually point to the domestic capitalists rather than the "American imperialists" as the foremost enemy and insist that peaceful methods are more suited to bringing about their downfall than are violent ones.

Confrontations and splits have been developing in nearly every interest group and party throughout the "progressive" camp. As noted earlier, a number of the moderate socialists bolted the Socialist Party in 1959 to form a new Democratic-Socialist Party of their own. Within the Socialist Party, while the Leftists are numerically much the stronger, they have in turn split into the more flexible "Eda" and the more doctrinaire "Sasaki" groups. The Eda coalition succeeded in capturing the secretary-generalship in 1961 for Saburō Eda himself and in 1962 for his associate, Tomomi Narita. This faction has championed a program calling for "structural reform," that is, the socialization of the country, not by a frontal attack on capitalism, but by working within it to transform its structure. This theory was heavily influenced by the conceptions of the Italian Communist leader, Palmiro Togliatti. It calls for class struggle and fundamental change. On the other hand, it distinguishes the Japanese Socialists clearly from the Japanese Communists, for its attitude toward the capitalist enemy is more moderate than before, placing a higher value on parliamentary action; and it has been coupled with a foreign policy doctrine of a more "positive neutralism." In the Sino-Soviet dispute it is the Soviet position that has, in general, attracted its sympathy. But the Sasaki-led Left denounces "structural reform," champions extra-parliamentary action and follows the "Chinese line"; and it is this wing that now dominates.

The "peace movement," which has appealed more widely perhaps than any other interest group in Japanese history, has experienced this same tendency. Moderate socialists and humanitarians of various political persuasions have found it increasingly uncomfortable to be associated in a movement that the Communists sought always to turn to their own purposes. In 1961, a number of moderate socialists pulled out of the *Gensuikyō* (Japan Society Against Atomic and Hydrogen Bombs) to form their own anti-bomb organization which is now closely affiliated with the Democratic-Socialist Party. At the VIIIth and IXth World Congresses Against Atomic and Hydrogen Bombs in the summers of 1962 and 1963, when the Communist leadership blocked resolutions condemning the resumption of nuclear tests equally by the Soviet Union and the United States, the Socialist Party and *Sōhyō* delegates stalked out; and in the summer of 1964 they held their own rival anti-bomb rally.

In the labor movement, the moderate federation known as *Zenrō* (All-Japan Congress of Trade Unions), backing the Democratic-Socialist Party, succeeded in April 1962 in persuading two other smaller labor federations to join it in forming a Japan United Congress of Labor, the *Dōmei Kaigi*, which, while having only 1,400,000 members in contrast to *Sōhyō's* 3,800,000, will give moderate trade unionism a more powerful center than before. Within *Sōhyō* itself moderation seems to be growing. Since the summer of 1962, for example, it has reaffirmed in convention its determination to support only the Socialist Party and not the Communist Party and has eased up on the political struggles it had been stressing since 1958, tending to concentrate on economic struggles of immediate concern to Japanese workers. But there are no signs that *Sōhyō* and *Dōmei Kaigi* might be able to work together.

Thus, the progressive camp seems to be rocked by confrontations between extremist and moderate elements in each of its organizations, the outcome of which is not clearly foreseeable. Nor is it apparent, therefore, how, in the event of a progressive majority at the polls, a government of progressives could readily be formed.

It must also be noted that the slow increase in the popularity of progressivism is accompanied by a parallel increase in the activity and even popularity of the extreme Right. Already the activists are almost as numerous as before the war and already they have shown in the Asanuma incident in 1960 and in the Shimanaka incident in 1961 that they are prepared to engage in political and cultural terrorism as before.

Less shocking but perhaps more significant than the revival of terrorism has been the rapid growth of the *Sōka Gakkai*, a new movement among the more poorly educated and underprivileged members of society. *Sōka Gakkai* is a faith-healing branch of the militant Nichiren sect of Buddhism. With a rapidly expanding membership today of more than two and one-half million households, it has entered the political lists, winning its members away from the "progressives" and marshaling their votes—over four million of them in the House of Councillors election in the summer of 1962—for its own candidates. Although it calls for no revision of the anti-war article of the Japanese Constitution and, in that sense, has some affinity with "progressivism," its major emphasis would seem to be on the dominant role that religion should play in politics, and that is a traditional appeal to the right even of Japanese "conservatism." It would therefore be rash indeed to feel sure that the forces of traditional reactionary nationalism have been spent and will not rise to block the progressive drift.

More perhaps than anything else, what makes a progressive takeover most uncertain is the future development of Japanese conservatism. There is some evidence that the alignment factions are going more extremist, sharpening the conflict with progressives, calling for firm adherence to the alliance, a settlement with South Korea, and a strengthening of the ties with the Chinese government on Taiwan. At least one leader, Shigeru Yoshida, has spoken of an eventual need for nuclear weapons. It may be that these policies will increasingly commend themselves to the Japanese people as prosperity increases within the framework of alignment. On the other hand, it seems more likely that, as electoral support declines, the members of the Liberal-Democratic Party will seek to check the trend to progressivism by taking up some of the progressives' issues.

35

This might well bring about a shift in the balance of power within the Party, leading to a transfer of leadership to the "independence factions," whose position is closest to that of the neutralist progressives. Whether this reformulation of Japanese conservatism could be successful is difficult to predict. If it were not, one supposes there would be strong pressure among these "independence factions" to split off and seek a coalition with moderate socialists, thus splitting the progressive movement altogether.

In short, while the next ten years may bring a progressive victory, this is by no means certain. In any event, their growing popularity seems bound within the next few years to provoke some significant changes in the Liberal-Democratic Party, possibly causing it to modify its leadership and its policies or to split in an effort to prevent a clear progressive victory. Thus, whatever the future of Japanese politics, whether it brings victory to the progressives, new leadership to the conservatives, or a middle-of-the-road conservative-progressive coalition, the trend of foreign policy seems most likely to be away from alignment and toward greater independence if not toward neutralism.

It is for this trend that America must prepare itself.

THE KOREAN QUANDARY

Across the Japan Sea and jutting down from a hostile mainland is the Korean peninsula. On its tip live the South Koreans, half a nation of poor and confused people who are struggling to build an independent state and a free society against enormous odds.

The Korean people like to say that they go back thousands of years, perhaps as many as 3,000, to a legendary age when a lengendary Chinese founder brought order to the peninsula. Whether or not this is true, historical records do go back more than 1,500 years and allow us to trace the growth of a unique, homogeneous culture, many features of which persist to the present. The majority of the people, for example, still live in rural villages much as they did a hundred or a thousand years ago, their homes built primarily of clay and straw, the drudgery of farm work or the darkness of night unrelieved by electricity, their diet made up primarily of vegetables, made tasty by the aromatic *kimchi* pickle, their lives a local round of toil. Here the children and the adults have learned to live together according to very old precepts laid down originally by Confucius and then elaborated on by his followers in China and Korea. Here also they have learned how to live with superiors. Deference toward superiors has always underlain their attitude toward political life, for the country has been divided traditionally into two groups of people: the farming class, which has lived a relatively secluded existence and has had little to do with the central affairs of the country; and a very small, aristocratic, urban, educated elite, which has monopolized literacy and governed the country according to Confucian precepts.

These traditional ideas upon which Korean society is based were seriously threatened only a hundred years ago by the coming of the West. The existence of Korea had been known to the West long before that, but during the period when Westerners were moving to India, Southeast Asia, China and finally Japan, the Koreans had steadfastly kept their borders sealed. It was not, in fact, until 1876, after the Western states had failed, that Japan was able to force Korea to open its doors. The United States was next, in 1882, managing to obtain the right to send in diplomatic representatives. As a result, Korea suddenly became the object of attention of a number of foreign diplomats, businessmen, missionaries and naval officers, who brought with them ideas of individualism, capitalism, militarism and highly centralized political systems.

Some Koreans of the younger generation were attracted by these exotic ideas and tried to change their ancient society in accordance with them; they looked eagerly to the West and Japan. On the other hand, most Korean leaders, particularly those of the older generation, who had grown up with Confucian teachings and had enjoyed the fruits of their privileged position, opposed the West and opposed change on its model. For twenty-five years, rather than adapting themselves, they clung to their old ways, with the result that Korea fell under the influence of first one country and then another, until finally, in 1910, it became a colony in the Empire of Japan.

For thirty-five years thereafter the Koreans lived as subjects of Japan. This was the situation that faced the Allies in 1945, when the Soviet Union sent in its troops from the north and the Americans sent in their troops from the south. Flying in to the old abandoned Japanese airfields, the Americans and Soviets were greeted with wild cries of liberation. A powerful spirit of patriotism swept through the land as Koreans from all walks of life pledged themselves to recover their heritage and reshape it into a modern, independent and democratic country. The Allies shared this purpose. Already in 1943 at Cairo President Roosevelt, China's President Chiang Kai-shek and Britain's Prime Minister Winston Churchill had agreed that in due course Korea should be free and independent. Thus, in the summer of 1945 the words on everyone's lips in Korea were independence, freedom and unity.

Today these words have a bitter taste. Everywhere in Korea there is dependence, dictatorship and division. It is important to understand why.

I. NORTH KOREA

The division of the country at the 38th parallel between North and South stems from 1945, when that line was chosen as a convenient demarcation of the zone in which the Russian forces would accept the surrender of the Japanese and that in which the U. S. would do the same. It was perpetuated and hardened by the inability of the two "liberating" countries to agree on the structure of a unified Korea and the subsequent formation, in 1948, of two competing, hostile regimes.

North of the line of division and occupying a little more than half the peninsula live about ten million, or one-third, of the Korean people. They are governed by the North Korean Workers Party, which embraces about 13 per cent of the population in a totalitarian party of Communist style and ideology, modeled on the Communist Party of the Soviet Union but today inclined toward and associated with the Chinese leadership in Peking. Native leadership was originally provided by factions of national Communists, who had carried on partisan activities in Korea during the years of Japanese rule, Moscow Communists, who had spent their years abroad in training or partisan activity under Soviet direction, and Yenan Communists, who had worked with the Chinese. With Soviet backing, a young partisan fighter from the Manchurian border, Kim Il-sung, came to the top. Rival factions were systematically liquidated, the national Communists largely by 1953 and the Yenan faction largely by 1958, leaving Kim in uncontested Stalin-like control.

Kim and his Party rule through the government of the Democratic People's Republic of Korea, which was organized in 1948 on the Soviet model: a Premier, six Deputy Premiers, and a Cabinet, responsible to a Supreme People's Assembly elected every four years. In addition, they have created a powerful apparatus of mass organizations, whose functions are to mobilize each sector of the population, such as labor, youth, women, students and farmers, in support of the Party's programs. Finally, they command, in addition to police forces, a modernized ground army of 340,000 men, a MIG-equipped air force of perhaps 1,000 planes, and a small navy of 170 ships. Of these forces, some 150,000 ground forces are believed to be held in combat readiness along the truce line facing South Korea.

Little is known from direct objective observation about life in North Korea; but the general trend of the statistics released by the regime itself are confirmed by the observations of visiting Japanese reporters. An industrialized, socialized society is the regime's domestic goal; it seems well on its way to achieving that. Nearly all economic activity seems to have been brought under government ownership or control. The traditional family plots of farmland have been reorganized into collective farms, the amount of land under cultivation has been enlraged, grain production has been increased and other agricultural activities have been expanded. Mining and industrial output in such lines as cement, steel, textiles and food processing industries has been greatly increased and electric power output per capita has almost come to equal that of Japan. The emphasis has been on the production of heavy industrial, rather than consumer, goods, but one of the most competent American students of the Korean scene concludes that "the people of North Korea are better fed and clothed and housed than ever before in their history."

Externally, the North Koreans have few contacts outside the Communist bloc. Other than Communist states, only Guinea and Mali have fully recognized their government, although India, Indonesia and Burma have established consular relations, and Iraq, Egypt and Austria have official trade relations. Inevitably, their foreign policy has been directed at maintaining the closest possible ties with their two big neighbors, the Soviet Union and Communist China, from each of which they have received extensive cultural, economic, military and political support, and upon whose continued support their survival depends.

Their ambition, of course, is to reunify Korea under Communist rule. Following the abortive military assault on South Korea in 1950 and the armistice in 1953, their program for achieving this has been to secure first the withdrawal of all foreign forces from both sides, then the formation of an all-Korea commission in which each regime would be equally represented and all decisions would need to be unanimous, and finally the holding of elections throughout Korea under the supervision of a neutral nations supervisory commission. Following the military coup in the South in 1961, the North Korean government added a new condition. Before unification could now be considered, South Koreans would have to overthrow the military junta and place in control a united front of Communists and their sympathizers.

II. SOUTH KOREA

South of the truce line live a much larger Korean population of 25 million, packed densely into an area slightly smaller than that of the North. Here under American occupation from 1945 to 1948 a variety of political parties were formed, none being a truly national organization, but each representing factional support among the Korean elite for one or another leader of the Korean independence movement abroad, whether a Christian educator, a lesser official from the era of Japanese rule, or some other notable. The demand for immediate independence was strong, and most political groups called for the early evacuation of American and Soviet troops and the establishment of a united government for all Korea; but a few, notably the faction led by Syngman Rhee, a strongly conservative man of the old aristocracy, who had spent most of his life in the United States as a propagandist for Korean independence, reconciled themselves to the Soviet-American impasse, accepted the bitter fact that the powers would not unite the country, and recommended that an independent government be sought for South Korea alone. As the United States was drawn to this same solution, Rhee gained greater power.

The first general election of the Republic of Korea was held in 1948 under UN auspices. The North Korean regime, however, refused to cooperate and the leftists and moderates in South Korea joined the boycott, with the result that control in the new Assembly fell to the rightist parties who, in turn, elected Syngman Rhee President. From that time on Rhee and his associates worked unceasingly to secure absolute control. In 1951 supporting factions were finally organized into a Liberal Party. In 1952 martial law was declared and physical force was used to compel the legislature to amend the Constitution to permit the President to be popularly elected. He was re-elected and in 1954 succeeded for the first time in securing the election of Liberal Party men to a majority of the Assembly seats. In 1956 force was again resorted to in order to amend the Constitution, permitting Rhee to run a third time. He won this election as well; but, when his Party's running mate for the vice presidency, Yi Ki-bu, was defeated by John M. Chang (Chang Myŏn) of the Democratic Party, Rhee forced through the legislature in 1958 a National Security Law and twenty-two other bills giving him almost dictatorial powers over all opposition and the right to appoint local officials who had previously been elected. As a result, in a completely controlled election in March 1960, Rhee and Lee swept the field, but not without violence, the police killing some ten persons and wounding at least forty more in a bloody melee at Masan.

When the body of a seventeen-year-old schoolboy, missing since the election day riots, was found a few weeks later, on April 11, with evidences of police brutality, public resentment boiled over. A violent riot ensued as students attacked government and Liberal Party buildings and the homes of Party leaders. Popular wrath focused on Yi Ki-bu as the chief organizer of the election, and a new election was demanded. A week later, on April 18, high school and university students all over the land carried out orderly mass demonstrations against police interference in elections. The following day the students of Seoul marched on the presidential palace. The populace cheered, the army held back, the government and its hated police were isolated. On April 27 Rhee resigned. The following day Yi Ki-bu and his family committed suicide. Thus ended the April Revolution and the long dictatorial reign of Syngman Rhee and his Liberal Party.

New elections were held after the Constitution was amended once again and the Second Republic was inaugurated. The conservative opposition factions, loosely grouped in the Democratic Party, came to power, led by the weak but liberally inclined Chang Myŏn. Public expectations were high as true civil freedom came to Korea for the first time; but Chang's government had barely begun to tackle Korea's problems when it was ousted on May 16, 1961, by a bloodless military coup. At 4 a.m. about 250 officers leading 3,800 armed men moved into Seoul and without opposition seized control of all government organs. South Korea passed quietly under military dictatorship. The Constitution was set aside and power exercised by a military junta, led by General Park Chung-hee, styled formally the Chairman of the Supreme Council for National Reconstruction.

Born in a farm village in South Korea in 1917, Park prepared for a career as a primary school teacher. In 1940 he was selected by the Japanese Army for training first at its Military Academy in Manchukuo, then in Tokyo, after which he received his commission in the Japanese Imperial Army. He continued his military career under the American occupation, attending the Korean Military Academy. During the Korean War he rose to the rank of Brigadier General, after which he attended an advanced course in the U.S. Army Artillery School at Fort Sill, Oklahoma. By 1960 he was deputy commanding general of the ROK Second Army.

The junta was not ambitious on its own behalf, Park declared. It sought only to eliminate political corruption, strengthen the anti-Communist front and start the country on the road to economic self-support; this done, it would return the country to civilian, constitutional rule. The United States, which was deeply committed to the defense of South Korea, felt it had been betrayed, but it established a working relationship with the new regime when it promised to hold general elections not later than May 1963.

Martial law was established. The Prime Minister and the Cabinet were arrested. The National Assembly and all local assemblies were closed. All political parties were disbanded. The civilian bureaucracy was purged. Military officers were attached to every government office. Schools were policed. Mass media were supervised. The dictatorship was complete. A puritanical moral reform campaign was launched, patriotic sentiments were stirred and an economic plan was widely publicized. In December 1962, in anticipation of the restoration of civilian government, a new Constitution was submitted to popular referendum and approved; it provided for a popularly elected National Assembly and a President elected by direct ballot.

At first the population was docile. The farmers gave the new regime support, even though intellectuals were more cautious. Strong and positive backing, however, failed to materialize. By the winter of 1962-63, when political parties were again permitted to function and plans were needed for the promised elections in the spring, unemployment was high and public confidence low. It could hardly be said that the junta had succeeded in reforming the political life of the nation or in setting it positively on the path of economic development. Many in the regime, including General Park, felt that it would be a mistake to turn over power under such uncertain conditions. At least four more years of junta rule, and then two additional years of military-civilian coalition, were needed, in the junta's view, before a necessary degree of stability could be achieved. On the other hand, the former civilian political leaders would not be put off, and the United States backed them. Finally a compromise was struck: elections on October 15, the transfer of power on December 26.

In the ensuing months General Park resigned from the armed forces to campaign as candidate of his specially formed Democratic Republican Party. He appealed particularly to the farmers, whose lot the junta had worked hard to alleviate with fertilizer distribution, help in irrigation, easing of loan requirements, and other aids. Various dissident ex-junta members and elderly civilian leaders of the former political factions sought to rally the opposition. In the end, five opposing names remained on the ballot, but the leading figure among them was the candidate of the Civil Rule Party, Yun Po-sŏn, sixty-seven, Presbyterian, Western-educated, former president of the Republic.

The campaign was spirited and the election apparently one of the most free in Korean history. General Park, winning about 46.65 per cent of the votes, emerged the victor over Yun by the very slim plurality of less than 2 per cent of the valid votes cast. His party did even less well in the election to the National Assembly one month later, when it gleaned only 33.5 per cent of the popular vote, much of which came from the rural southernmost provinces where Park himself came from. Again, however, the opposition parties had been unable to unite and instead had put forward a large number of competing candidates, with the result that the next most successful party, Yun Po-sŏn's Civil Rule Party, won only 20 per cent of the vote.

Clearly Park and his followers had only minority support in the nation. On the other hand, the effect of the elections was to put them firmly in the saddle. Under the new Constitution, in addition to the representatives elected from each district, each party is given a number of seats proportionate to the size of its national vote. As a consequence, the weak popular showing of Park's Democratic Republican Party was overcome in the Assembly seats secured, so that the DRP won 110 seats out of a total of 175, or a majority of 62 per cent.

When the Third Republic was inaugurated on December 17, 1963, it brought some new faces to Seoul. The Assembly was distinguished by being younger, more inexperienced and with a higher percentage of reserve officers than any previous legislature. But a number of the leaders of the military regime remained. A disproportionate number of officials of the new government were drawn from Park's home region in the south; and two familiar faces remained prominent in the line-up of power: President Park himself, of course, and also his brother-in-law, Brigadier General Kim Chong-p'il, one of the chief planners of the military coup in 1961, head of the intelligence organs under the military regime, and first chairman of the ruling Democratic Republican Party.

The transition to constitutional government was gratifying to supporters of democracy; but the opposition, led by students and former civilian politicians, continues unreconciled. In spring 1964 they seized on the issue of Japanese-Korean relations, which the government was promoting, to demonstrate again in the streets forcing the negotiations with Japan to be terminated and General Kim to resign and leave the country. Moreover, the fundamental question remained: could that government at last marshal the energies of the nation to solve the extraordinarily difficult problems that confronted it?

III. SOME FUNDAMENTAL PROBLEMS

The reasons for political instability in South Korea are many, and some are fundamental:

1. *Defense.* The problem of defending the ROK against its northern neighbors is obvious and one to which the United States has given major attention. During the period of Occupation, from 1945 to 1948, the United States guaranteed the security of South Korea by the presence of its own military forces; but, in 1949, shortly after the formation of the Republic of Korea, these forces were withdrawn as part of a broader policy of military pull-back from Asia. American strategic planners felt at the time that the Korean peninsula was not essential to American security and were prepared for disengagement and the end of active defense of South Korea. Only a military training mission was left behind. As a consequence, on June 25, 1950, the North Korean forces moved across the frontier in force, aiming to destroy the South Korean government and to reunify the land under their own control.

The invasion shocked the American government into an immediate re-evaluation of its policies. Overnight it pledged itself to the defense of the South. American forces played a major role in the bloody fighting that followed, as did those of South Korea, which were quickly built up to 600,000 men and further bolstered by contingents from many members of the United Nations. As a result, despite extensive support given them by the Communist Chinese, the North Koreans were driven back. An armistice was signed in July 1953, providing for an end to hostilities and the establishment of a narrow neutral zone roughly along the 38th parallel. Thereupon, the sixteen nations that had responded to the call of the United Nations to help defend the Republic pledged themselves to resist any further attack. In October 1953 the United States herself signed a mutual defense treaty with South Korea.

Since that time, while the United States has repatriated the bulk of its armed forces, it has retained a substantial contingent in Korea and has continued to supply the South Korean forces with their major needs. The military problem that remains is simply that no peace treaty has yet been signed. The two sides talk to each other regularly around the table in the little shed at Panmunjom, while armed men on both sides patrol the neutral zone and keep their powder dry. These conversations, however, have been futile and are likely to remain so. As long as North Korea has the close, unlimited military support of the Russians or the Chinese—and today it has the pledges of both—there is no way for South Korea to become militarily self-sufficient. It can provide the manpower, but it cannot produce the weapons, other necessary supplies and advanced training; nor can it pay for them.

There is a second element in South Korea's military problem although it is impossible to be sure how serious it is: discipline. Until the military coup in 1961 the armed forces had been loyally obedient to the government and to the UN command. Since the coup they have dominated the political life of the nation. As a result, the higher officers seem to have fallen victim to the same kind of factionalism that has plagued the political parties and to have developed a taste for political power. No evidence of operational inefficiency has yet been reported, but from time to time high-ranking officers have been arrested on charges of plotting to overthrow the government. Between the government and the UN Command, serious efforts have been made to restore confidence. In January 1965 the government responded favorably to the American appeal for South Korean troops to be sent to South Vietnam; and in the spring the UN Command approved the movement of Korean forces to help quell the riotous demonstrations of those seeking to use the Japan issue to bring down the government.

2. *The Economy.* South Korea is an underdeveloped country that has not yet "taken off" on the path to industrialization. Most of its population is rural, farming small plots in the manner of their ancestors. The number of mouths to be fed, however, grows at the rate of nearly 3 per cent per annum, which constitutes one of the

highest rates in the world and results in South Korea's being one of the most densely populated lands on earth, having more than 650 persons per square mile. Rural poverty is intense; many persons stream into the cities looking for work, thus joining the destitute refugees who poured down from the North during the civil war. Unfortunately, there has been little urban work for them. The minerals needed for manufacturing industries are to be found largely in the North, and there is no trade between the two Koreas. Private capital is small and prefers commercial speculation to industrial entrepreneurship. Trade deficits are endemic. Economic planning by the government has been faulty, and American economic aid has not been used as wisely as it might have been.

As a result, when the military took over the government in 1961, unemployment stood at approximately 10 per cent of the population. An ambitious five-year plan was drawn up for the period 1962 to 1967, aiming at fundamental improvements in agriculture, the development of heavy and chemical industries, the expansion of electric power production, and the promotion of exports, so that the over-all rate of growth might be raised to 7.1 per cent annually. Some progress was made, particularly in the area of import restriction and rural credit, but the necessary capital has not been found, either at home or abroad, to make the plan genuinely operative. Prices continue to rise and economic hardships to grow.

3. *Leadership.* These problems would be difficult for any people to solve, but the Korean population has been peculiarly ill-equipped to deal with them. By 1945 the Japanese had given elementary education to a proportion of the population, but had left the bulk of it illiterate; only 22 per cent of those over twelve could read. Given the extraordinary devotion of the people to the ways of their fathers, this meant that change would prove extremely difficult to popularize and implement. It is a great tribute to the Korean people that, despite their many tribulations in the postwar period, they have given themselves wholeheartedly to education, with the result that today more than 85 per cent have achieved literacy and an impressive number have received a higher education. They are ready now as never before to respond to enlightened leadership.

But such a leadership has not been forthcoming. When the Japanese left in 1945, no effective Korean leadership was ready to take over. Japanese authoritarianism had been too thorough. Under Japanese rule the sentiment for independence had never been able to crystallize into an effective political movement through which ambitious young Koreans could learn the arts of persuasion, compromise, organization and popular leadership. There was no political party, like the Indian Congress Party, for example, ready to take over when the Japanese surrendered. Nor were there men of wide practical experience in any field other than Christian education, for the Japanese had effectively kept top leadership positions in nearly every field of endeavor for themselves.

The men who vied for leadership in this vacuum were of three types. There were those who had worked with the Japanese, had accepted their education and had risen through their favor to middle-level positions in local administration, the courts, the police, etc. Inevitably, they had absorbed many of the authoritarian attitudes of prewar Japanese colonial administrators, feeling that the bureaucracy should dominate the government, and that the government should dominate the people, the police being the logical instrument of that domination. Another group of potential leaders were those Koreans who had been educated in Christian colleges in Korea or in the West, who had acquired a certain facility in manipulating Western ideas and dealing with foreigners, and had some experience in Korean social and religious organizations; but they had little or no experience in practical government and in many cases had little or no contact with the illiterate or poorly educated, tradition-oriented masses of the people. Finally, there were the revolutionaries, the agitators for independence who had spent most of their adult lives overseas, propagandizing the cause of Korean independence and competing with each other for leadership; their experience fitted them for subversion and intrigue, but hardly for responsible policy-making, the leadership of mass parties, or effective administration.

These then were the men who sought to lead the nation, with the results already described: a twelve-year period of authoritarian rule by a corrupt administration under Syngman Rhee, from 1948 to 1960, and an ineffective second try for one year under Chang Myŏn. Inevitably, the rising younger generation grew more and more dissatisfied. Its frustration found expression first in the student revolution of 1960; but, of course, the students were not equipped by either age or experience to take over, and, indeed, they had no intention of doing so. Their action served simply to clear away the aging Liberal Party group of civilian leaders, thus permitting another group of older civilians of fundamentally similar origins and mentality, the Democrats under Chang Myŏn, to take over. The latter also failed to inspire the younger generation with their leadership.

While, therefore, civilian leaders have largely failed to develop, a modern military leadership has come into being, largely because of the Korean war and the extensive assistance of the United States. A few young Koreans were given officer training by the Japanese in the 1940's. These few, supplemented by thousands more in the years after 1945, were put through Korean military schools, given advanced training in the United States, hardened in combat, and matured during command experience. The officer corps of the South Korean armed forces has thus become the most modernized, most disciplined and best organized leadership group in the country. It is small wonder that, as civilian politicians faltered a second time, a nucleus of ambitious and patriotic young officers seized control.

Regrettably, however, the military life did not train these men in the political arts, nor did it give them broad knowledge and skill in economic affairs. They have not themselves known how to get the country on its feet, and by their authoritarianism they have temporarily at least frustrated the development of an alternative young civilian leadership, either in the government bureaucracy or in the public at large. This then may be the most fundamental problem of all: how to provide the social environment in which new, more capable leaders can be trained and eventually brought to power.

IV. AMERICA'S STAKE

For these and other reasons, South Korea has made little progress. It has remained politically unstable and economically prostrate. Its army has grown strong, but its discipline has become questionable. Only a few of the states of the world have recognized it. The day when it can be more than a ward of the United States not only has not dawned but cannot now be foreseen. Yet, in spite of South Korea's tragic weakness, the United States has consistently backed it, with the blood of its citizens in the Korean war and with $5 billion in economic and military aid, accounting annually for about 75 per cent of the military budget, about 50 per cent of the civil budget, and about 80 per cent of available foreign exchange.

The basic reasons for this extensive American commitment cannot be found in Korea itself or in the importance of Korea to the United States. After all, politically, militarily, economically and culturally it has been a net drain on American resources. Rather, the basic reasons are to be found, first of all, in America's stand for collective security. Since the Republic of Korea was established in 1948 under the auspices of the United Nations, and since its life was defended in the Korean war under the banner of the United Nations as a matter of collective security, its continued existence is vital to the prestige of the world body and the principle of collective security.

Secondly, this commitment is part of America's policy of building and maintaining a world front against the expansion of Communist influence and control. In this, the vitality of the Korean regime is important to our campaign to persuade other "new" or "newly emerging" peoples that independence, democracy and economic growth are not only desirable, but reasonable objectives, and that if they associate closely with America and other free Western societies, they may attain these objectives more surely and more speedily than might otherwise be the case. And the vitality of our military protection is important if our other allies are to retain their confidence in us.

Thirdly, South Korea is important to us also because it is important to Japan, our most important ally in that part of the world. These two countries have been intimately associated throughout history, but increasingly so in modern times. Neither can be indifferent to the fate of the other. Were America to withdraw, thereby inviting the collapse of the South Korean regime and its absorption by North Korea, that event would have serious limiting effects on Japan's long-range economic development, place greater burdens on Japan's defense forces than they are now prepared to assume, and would intensify the strains between the Left and Right in Japan, with results it is not now possible to foresee.

So long as the Republic holds fast to its principle of independence, its insistence on unification with the North only on the basis of free elections, and its dream of economic development and political democracy, it seems likely that the American people will continue to want to help. The difficult question is really, how *can* we help? Grants for survival are necessary, but they do not satisfy a deeper urge felt in both South Korea and the United States to get to the bottom of Korea's troubles and begin to build for a new life. If we are ever to satisfy this urge, we must tackle the problems which are fundamental as well as those which are current, and we must be patient, for solutions to Korea's fundamental problems will take a long time indeed.

The Korean quandary is first and most fundamentally a problem for the Koreans, but it is more than that. Korea is the eye of the storm in Northeast Asia, the vortex of the confrontation of Soviet, Chinese, Japanese and American power. The resolution of the quandary is therefore of vital concern to all.

There can be no doubt that the solution which has greatest appeal to the Korean people is reunification. If the factories, the water power and the minerals of the North could be integrated with the farms and surplus population of the South, a far more self-supporting economy would be possible and the prospects for sustained economic development relatively bright. Moreover, Korea is not a synthetic nation. It is one of the oldest nations in the world, with a strong racial homogeneity, a rich cultural heritage and a long political identity. Its division since 1945 has dismembered not only the body but the psyche of the nation as well. The pain of the wound can be assuaged, but it is unlikely that it can be healed finally by any remedy short of reunification.

It is therefore important to understand clearly why reunification has not come about. The first reason is the attitude of the two governments. The history of the North is that of the steady consolidation of power by Kim Il Sung; and he has insisted that reunification not be bought at the price of sacrificing the power of his regime. The conservative regimes in the South have been equally intransigent, insisting that only the Republic is the legitimate government of all Korea. There have, however, been other voices. During the period of the American Military Government from 1945 to 1948 there were many political leaders who insisted that unification must come first. They included not only the Communists, organized as the South Korean Labor Party, but also the non-Communist left under Lyuh Un-hyong and many moderates and right-wingers, such as Kim Kyu-sik and Kim Ku. Most of them were eliminated in the course of the bitter struggles accompanying Syngman Rhee's rise to power; the Labor Party, for example, was banned in 1947 and Lyuh and Kim Ku were assassinated.

In 1956 the conciliatory policy found a new southern champion in Cho Bong-am, former Vice-Speaker of the Assembly and head of a new Progressive Party. In 1958 the Party was banned and Cho was arrested; a year later he was hanged on charges of espionage; but the idea of a negotiated reunification was not crushed. In fact, it raised its head again following the student revolt of 1960. With civil liberties restored by the government of Chang Myŏn, a number of new political parties as well as young people generally began urging that students North and South by-pass their governments and themselves go to Panmunjom to confer on unification. A Students Association for National Reunification was organized in seventeen universities, and demonstrations were held in many cities. The police eventually brought the students under control, but General Park used their actions as one of the reasons justifying his seizure of power in April 1961. Since then he has exercised extremely close surveillance over the students and all intellectuals. Indeed, when one realizes that this movement took place in spite of the long years of anti-Communist indoctrination and the bitter memories of the civil war, one is driven to the conclusion that the sentiment for reunification still runs strong and that there is a powerful undercurrent in Korean society, chiefly among the intellectuals, for abandoning the southern Republic and conceding what may be necessary to bring about reunification with the North. It seems likely that there is a similar current in the North, but of that nothing is known.

The second major obstacle to reunification has been the attitude of the powers: the Soviet Union and Communist China on the one side, and the United States on the other. Chinese interest in Korea goes back many centuries. It was in fact only defeat in the Sino-Japanese War in 1894-95 that forced the Chinese to abandon their traditional, privileged position. The strategic use made of the peninsula by Japan in its continental expansion over the next fifty years served only to strengthen the Chinese conviction of Korea's importance to them; and in 1950, although the People's Government of China was hardly a year old, it poured its "volunteers" across the Yalu to hold North Korea for a friendly regime. It seems to have withdrawn its forces in 1954, but it has pledged its readiness, under the Treaty of Mutual Defense of 1961, to return to the aid of North Korea whenever needed; and it has extended significant economic aid. Under the conditions of the Sino-Soviet split, it may be presumed that Peking would prefer not to become militarily involved in Korea; on the other hand, it must look on the control of North Korea by a friendly regime as even more important than before.

Russian interest in Korea is not of such long duration as Chinese, but in modern times it has been almost equally intense. Particularly between 1895 and 1905 Russia sought to succeed to China's hegemony in the peninsula and was prevented only by Japanese arms in the Russo-Japanese War of 1904-5. Like the Chinese, the Russians had good reason in view of the Siberian Expedition and Japan's continental expansion thereafter to assign to Korea a very high strategic value. Their support of the North Koreans during the Korean civil war, their Mutual Defense Treaty of 1961, their economic aid and their continuing support for North Korean unification testify to the strength of Soviet concern. It seems likely that they would not want, any more than Peking, an embroglio in Korea while Sino-Soviet relations are so tense; but there is little to support the view that they would be prepared to stand by were the security of the North Korean regime threatened.

The United States has been equally strong in supporting the division. Unlike the Soviets, it used its own forces to defend its southern client; and unlike the Chinese, it has kept these forces on the front line ever since. Its massive military and economic aid, its Mutual Defense Treaty of 1954, and its unwavering support of the Republic of Korea—all testify to its interest.

On the other hand, there are several policies that the United States has been pursuing in recent years which have begun to raise doubts in the minds of South Koreans about America's ultimate purposes. One is the reduction of aid.

Total American economic assistance to the Republic of Korea has been reduced from roughly $369 million in 1957 to $216 million in 1963, a reduction of 41 per cent (see Table 27). If surplus agricultural commodities imported under PL 480, Title 1, are subtracted from this, one finds that grant aid has been reduced even more sharply, from roughly $323 million in 1957 to $119 million in 1963, representing a cut of 63 per cent. American military assistance also has been reduced, from $230 million in 1961 to $141 million in 1964, and a projected $114 million in 1965 (see Table 28).

If this were a period of rapidly expanding exports and rising productivity, such reductions might be made with a minimum of political repercussions, but this is not the case. On the contrary, since 1960 Korea's overall trade deficit has remained high (in 1957 it was about $420 million, and in 1963 it rose to $473 million), while the bilateral deficit in the trade balance with the United States has grown substantially worse, climbing from $105 million in 1957 to $257 million in 1963. Meanwhile its GNP has done little more than keep up with the population growth, so that per capita income in 1962 was only U.S. $85, substantially the same as in 1958; and the unemployment level has hardened for several years at the high level of roughly 8.5 per cent.

There are, of course, many reasons for this freezing of the Korean economy, but it is not surprising that Koreans blame particularly the reduction in American aid. Intellectuals and government officials are aware of the reason given by the United States for its policy, namely, to ease its own serious balance of payments problem; but they are convinced that other reasons are more important. They believe that the United States is using its economic power to put pressure on the Park regime to get the soldiers out of politics, at first to restore, now to stabilize, constitutional rule by civilians. Beyond that is the fear that America is losing interest in Korea and may be preparing to withdraw, as it did diplomatically in 1905 and again, militarily, in 1949.

This latter fear is fed by developments in weapons technology and changes in strategic thinking in the United States, particularly as these suggest that America may be inclined in the future to rely more on long-range missiles and strategic strike forces and less on forward bases like those in South Korea. It is fed even more by the United States' policy of encouraging South Korea and Japan to resume relations.

Since the liberation of Korea in 1945 a cold war has been waged between the former colony and its defeated ruler. Investment has been liquidated, and trade has dropped to a fraction of its former value. Whereas in the late years of Japanese rule the trade between them accounted for almost one-third of Japan's total trade and more than three-quarters of that of Korea, today, according to Republic of Korea (ROK) statistics, less than one-third of its trade continues to be with Japan and, according to Japanese statistics, less than one-thirtieth of Japanese trade is with South Korea.

Political relations are even less flourishing. Indeed, after thirty-five years of the most intimate kind of political relations, neither of the two Korean regimes today has even regular diplomatic contacts with Japan. Their imperial relations were ended in 1945. By the San Francisco Treaty, which came into effect in April 1952, Japan accepted the independence of "Korea" and pledged itself to accept certain provisions concerning possible property claims, high seas fishery and trade involving "Korea"; but as in the case of China, no specific settlement of Korean-Japanese relations was provided and no Korean government was invited to be a signatory.

By the time the Japanese were freed to take up the problem of establishing a new relationship with "Korea," there were in fact two Koreas: the Democratic People's Republic in the North and the Republic in the South. Under the urging of the U.S. Occupation authorities, Japan did turn its attention to the South, opening negotiations in October 1951; but from the outset the talks did not go well. Six times broken off, the talks were resumed on December 3, 1964. This time they seem headed for success. On February 22, 1965, the Foreign Ministers of the two countries initialed a Draft Treaty on Basic Relations. On April 3 separate agreements on fishery, property claims and the legal status of Koreans also were signed. The main issues and the solutions achieved appear to be these:

1. The jurisdiction of the Government of the Republic of Korea. Like the governments of several other divided countries, the South Korean Government has consistently refused diplomatic relations with countries that have recognized its rival, in this case the North Korean regime.[1] The Government of the Republic of Korea insists that it is itself the only rightful government of all Korea, North as well as South. Many in South Korea feel that acknowledgment of this legitimacy must be secured from Japan in clear written form lest Japan later adopt a "two Koreas" policy, recognize the North as well, and thereby add a further obstacle to the achievement of the ROK's cherished objective: the unification of the peninsula under its own control. The Japanese government, on the other hand, has been loath to commit itself. To do so might make it liable to the Republic of Korea for property claims on behalf of all Korea, affect the legal status of Koreans in Japan (whom Japan has hitherto allowed to

[1] In November 1963 the South Korean Government made an exception of the United Arab Republic, retaining its Consulate General in Cairo in spite of Egypt's recognizing the Government of North Korea.

identify themselves with either the North or the South), antagonize the Communist bloc, including North Korea, and arouse the forces of the Japanese left, which champions the cause of the North. But in the Draft Treaty of February, Japan accepted the formula used by the UN General Assembly in 1948, confirming that "the Government of the Republic of Korea is the only lawful government of Korea."[2] At the same time it accepted another demand of the ROK, that the annexation treaties of 1910 and all earlier treaties between them were "already null and void."

2. The fixing of exclusive and joint fishery rights in waters around Korea. For years the Government of the Republic of Korea insisted on Japan's recognizing the so-called Rhee or Peace Line, according to which Korea claimed the right to exclude Japanese fishery from portions of the Sea of Japan as far as fifty miles offshore, and forcibly seized and detained Japanese violators. Japan denied the validity of the Line and vehemently protested the seizures. Little progress seems to have been made until 1961, when the representatives of the present Park Government in Seoul are reported to have acceded in general to Japan's demand that the line of exclusive Korean fishery be pulled back to roughly twelve miles off the Korean coast. On the other hand, the Koreans continue to insist that certain exceptions be made, particularly of the rich seas between the Korean peninsula and Cheju Island. The Korean argument for special rights in this area is that the harvest there is vitally important and the Korean fishery industry is too weak to compete equally with that of Japan; this same argument is used to justify its demand that Japan provide a fishery cooperation loan to help the Korean fishermen to modernize their equipment and their methods. In the agreement signed in April, most of the fishery problems appear to have been finally resolved. South Korea is reported to have agreed that the line of exclusive Korean fishery should follow the 12-mile limit in most instances, but Japan agreed that at least "for a certain period of time" a specified zone between Cheju and the mainland should be included.[3] Beyond this, they have agreed to a zone of joint fishery within which the fishermen of each country will be regulated as to size of catch and number of vessels employed. Finally, Japan has agreed to provide private credits of $90 million to help develop the South Korean fishing industry.

[2] *The Japan Times Weekly, international* edition, February 27, 1965.
[3] *Ibid.,* April 3, 1965.

3. Property claims. At the outset of the talks, the Japanese claimed the restitution of many properties that they had held before 1945 or compensation for their loss. The ROK Government insisted that Japan had given up all such rights by the San Francisco Treaty. Finally in 1957 the United States expressed the same opinion and Japan dropped its claims, but not before the ROK regime had drawn up counter-claims of its own, demanding compensation for losses sustained under the annexation and in the period of Japanese evacuation. These have been the subject of much dispute, for to the Koreans the payment of these claims is looked on as Japan's acknowledgment of its guilt, symbolically if not in actual measure, in exploiting Korea under the annexation. Japan's negotiators, on the other hand, have not been willing to proceed on this assumption. In 1953 the third attempt at negotiations was in fact broken off by the Koreans when the Japanese delegate, Kanichiro Kubota, questioned the reality of such exploitation. Now at last a measure of agreement seems to have been achieved. Japan is reported to have agreed to pay $300 million in property claims, and $200 million in intergovernmental economic cooperation loans, and an additional loan of $300 million on a private basis. The practical importance of these or similar sums, of course, is that they would make a major contribution to Korea's economic development and also to its trade financing.

4. Legal status of Korean residents in Japan. Koreans began moving to Japan late in the nineteenth century, but the exodus became particularly marked in the early 1940s when large numbers were brought to Japan as forced labor in support of the war. Probably more than two million at their height, many fled home in the chaotic early surrender period. By 1948 only some 600,000 were left. Those remaining were treated at first as Japanese nationals; but in 1950 Japan changed its policy. Thereafter all Koreans who resided in Japan prior to 1945 were permitted to become permanent residents; all others were classified as aliens. For a number of years the ROK Government took little interest in these Koreans in Japan, many of whom were impoverished and the victims of various forms of discrimination. Its only concern seemed to be to refuse to accept repatriation, especially of illegal entrants and criminals Japan was anxious to deport, unless each was allowed to bring out all his property and a sizable compensation. This the Japanese refused. Then, in 1959, the Japanese Government began to permit voluntary repatriation to the North; whereupon the ROK authorities became more deeply con-

cerned. Apparently alarmed by the adverse propaganda effect the repatriation was having on its interests in both Japan and South Korea, the ROK Government abruptly broke off all relations for a number of months in 1959 and 1960 and since then has been insisting that Japan must recognize it as the only homeland of all Korean aliens in Japan and therefore as the sole legitimate protector of the rights of all such Koreans, for whom a special status is claimed. Japan has usually answered that if Korean residents wish the welfare and other privileges of Japanese citizenship they should seek naturalization as Japanese; but in the agreement signed in April Japan did agree to grant the statutory privilege of permanent residence not only to those residents registering as South Korean nationals who have lived in Japan since before the surrender in 1945, but also to their direct descendants born within a five-year registration period and in turn to the second generation as well. It also agreed to limit the number of offenses for which Korean residents could be deported.

This leaves only the major issue:

5. Jurisdiction over the island of Dokdo or Takeshima, a barren group of islets and surrounding reefs, less than a tenth of a square mile, lying between the two countries far out in the Sea of Japan. Of no value, they are nevertheless claimed by both Japan and South Korea, and have become such a prestige issue that to the spring of 1965 no progress had been made toward settlement.

To most Americans and to a number of Koreans and Japanese as well, though probably a minority, these hostile relations are not only undesirable, but unnecessary. Japan and the Republic of Korea, they feel, are natural allies. They are separated only by relatively narrow straits. They have been intimately related for more than 1,500 years, Japan having imported many elements of its traditional culture from Korea and Korea having imported much of its modern culture from Japan. During the years of colonial rule, their economic relations were extremely strong. And today each is bound to the United States in common defense against Communist power. Now that Japan has recovered economically, would it not be a better solution to the Korean quandary—better, that is, than reunification with the North —for South Korea to turn to Japan, thereby stimulating a mutually beneficial flow of capital and goods? Might this not provide the impetus for the Korean economy at last to take off on the path of healthy development? Is it not reasonable to suppose also, as Japanese military power revives and as the Japanese people accept a greater concern for international security in the immediate region surrounding their own shores, that some mutually beneficial security arrangements also can be constructed between South Korea and Japan that would relieve both South Korea and the United States of some of the great military burdens they now bear and give Japan a greater, responsible scope for its power? For the time, the security possibilities of this Korea-Japan project have a very limited appeal, being chiefly to Americans and a few Japanese conservative military analysts; but the economic aspects have appealed more widely, to both the Park regime in Korea and the Ikeda and Sato Governments in Japan, and are the chief reason for the accelerated negotiations in recent years.

On the other hand, it is important to recognize the serious obstacles to the success of this project. Some of these are economic. After all, Korea is no longer under Japan's imperial control. No longer are the goods of each country traded duty-free in the markets of the other. No longer, through administration of the banking, transport, taxation and other institutions in Korea, is the Japanese government able to give this trade uniquely favorable treatment. No longer does Japan control the markets of North China, with which Korean development was also integrated. In addition, two prewar props have been lost: heavy Japanese investments in Korea and the sizable remittances to Korea from its several million nationals who were formerly overseas, particularly in Japan and Manchuria. Moreover, the economy of Japan has undergone such a striking change in structure and productivity since the war and its external economic relations have been so altered that its ability to absorb imports from Korea and its willingness to spare capital for investment there may have been seriously weakened. The trade has thus become partially dependent on Korea's ability to secure aid or investment from abroad.

Added to these material obstacles are equally serious problems of popular attitudes and politics. Among the Koreans there is great popular fear of a rivival of Japanese "economic aggression"; Japanese capital, raw materials and technical know-how are suspected as the carriers of economic imperialism, by which the hated exploitation of colonial days may be revived; and there is even deeper fear that any kind of security arrangements with Japan will result in Korean enslavement to the Japanese military. To the outsider these fears may seem pathological. But it is important to remember that American fears of Communism, for example, seem equally pathological to many non-Americans. These American fears are nonetheless very real and are powerful stimuli to action. Korean fears of Japan are equally real. The student riots in Seoul that disrupted Japanese-Korean talks in 1964 are eloquent testimony. It is understandable, therefore, that the American policy of urging the ROK Government to settle its differences with Japan and open its doors to Japanese trade and investment, coming as it does at the same time that the United States is reducing its own aid to Korea, both economic and military, is suspected by many Koreans of representing an American policy of withdrawing and turning the peninsula once again over to the Japanese; and if they feel that they must choose between reunification or the Japanese, some may well prefer reunification.

Among the Japanese, the elements opposing a settlement with South Korea include primarily the Communist and Socialist Parties and those leaders in the governing Liberal-Democratic Party who seek a rapprochement with Communist states, particularly People's China. The argument of the Socialists has been that a normalization of the relations between Japan and the Republic of Korea will perpetuate the conflict between South and North Korea, since it will antagonize the northern regime and place a new barrier in the way of "peaceful unification." Formal diplomatic relations, the Party has insisted, should not be established except with a unified government. For the time being it urges that Japan treat the regimes of North and South Korea equally, promoting trade and humane relations with each but recognizing neither. This, of course, is in accord with the general line of "positive neutrality" that the Socialist Party recommends for Japan.

Now it is true that the Socialist Party, even with the support on this issue of the Communist Party, does not have the backing of the majority of the Japanese people and does not have the strength in the Diet to block the passage of a Japan-ROK treaty; nevertheless it does have the power to disrupt the major cities, particularly Tokyo, with street demonstrations and to interfere with the Diet proceedings with boycotts, sit-downs and the like, so as to bring serious pressure to bear on the conservative leadership. The Ikeda and Sato governments have indicated that they are prepared to face that confrontation with the Left. On the other hand, there are also in the Liberal-Democratic Party those who believe such confrontations are unhealthy and should be avoided, those who believe Japan's major effort abroad should be to establish working relationships not with

63

South Korea but with the Communist powers, including mainland China, so that it can play an "independent" role as broker between East and West.

These various political party elements, strengthened by certain small businessmen organized in special trade associations, the giant labor federation, Sōhyō, the General Federation of Korean Residents in Japan, known as Chōsōren, and a number of other mass organization front groups, have been working for years to open up to Japan the North Korean option. Following the Geneva Conference in 1954, North Korea joined the Soviet Union and People's China in their campaign to persuade Japan to establish diplomatic relations and expand economic and cultural contacts. The Japanese Government responded with the imposition of a ban on direct trade with North Korea; nevertheless interested Japanese leaders succeeded privately in negotiating in October 1955 an unofficial trade agreement. A second unofficial trade agreement followed in February 1956, and since then a number of other so-called "people's agreements" have followed. In April 1961 the Ikeda government in Japan rescinded its ban on direct trade; and a direct shipping line was established between Osaka and Ch'ong-jin. The result has been an extremely modest (less than one-tenth of the Japan-South Korea trade) but nevertheless growing volume of trade, its value rising from approximately $8 million in 1961 to nearly $15 million in 1963 (see Table 36).

In 1958 a second campaign was launched from the North with even greater effect: the campaign to repatriate Korean residents in Japan to the North at North Korean expense. Heralded by the authorities in P'yongyang and Chōsōren in Japan, the movement captured the imagination not only of the usual North Korean supporters and the Left, but of the great bulk of the Japanese populace and finally the major parties, conservative as well as progressive. The "P'yongyang lobby" had its special purposes, of course, but many other Japanese seem to have been attracted by the possibility that free repatriation might relieve Japan of at least some of the Korean minority, which most Japanese found troublesome. Other Japanese, who felt a certain sense of guilt toward the Koreans, found some relief in supporting what to them seemed to be a humane undertaking. Still others found it acceptable as a way for Japan to play the kind of independent role in the world they wished for it, a role of dealing even-handedly with Communist as well as non-Communist countries. And it is not unlikely that a few looked on it as a way of bringing pressure to bear on the South Korean representatives in the perennial negotiations.

At last, early in 1959, Premier Kishi agreed to cooperate, and under the aegis of the Red Cross, so as to avoid political implications, the repatriation was begun. The authorities in Seoul were furious, but helpless, as the agreement has been several times extended, permitting more than 80,000 to leave Japan for a new life in North Korea.

The growing trade, the successful repatriation and the generally favorable reports of conditions in North Korea sent back by the Korean returnees and Japanese reporters have combined to give the Japanese people a more attractive image of the Northern regime than the Southern. They are also well aware that the North enjoys the support of the Soviet Union and People's China. Consequently most Japanese feel it desirable to keep open the door to North Korea, both for itself and for its relation to a larger desire, opening wider the door to mainland China. Few indeed are the Japanese who would jeopardize relations with mainland China for the sake of a settlement with South Korea. Were any Japanese government to go that far, it would certainly be shaken by opposition within its own party and confronted in the streets and in the Diet by a leftist assault of serious proportions.

Consequently, while the cold war between South Korea and Japan has weakened both countries and placed greater burdens on the United States, its resolution by treaty is unlikely without much disorder. In both Seoul and Tokyo opposition elements can be expected to take to the streets to try not only to block the ratification of the treaty, but also to topple the governments while Communists and other extremists aggravate anti-Americanism. Also, a treaty will be only a beginning. It will not produce immediately a close and effective relationship. That will take years of patient effort and probably cannot be achieved until the two countries can approach each other in some kind of equality and self-confidence; that is, not until the South Koreans are on their feet, with a growing economy, a stable polity and a confident society, and the Japanese are surer of the role they are to play in the world and more ready to bear the burdens a responsible role entails.

Meanwhile the role of the United States must be that of a good friend to each. If it would retain its Korean ally, it must expand rather than reduce its aid; it must render the best protection and advice it is capable of; and it must be prepared to stay until the Republic of Korea is well launched as a stable, prosperous and independent society. And if it would retain its Japanese ally, it must show understanding of the domestic political problems of Japan's leaders and respect for the judgment of these men as they seek a new and more independent place in the world community.

Part Two: REFERENCE

COMPILED WITH THE ASSISTANCE OF
SUNG HWAN CHANG

I. CHRONOLOGY OF KEY EVENTS

1945

August   Japan announces acceptance of the Allied terms of capitulation in the Potsdam Declaration and the war in the Pacific ends. Prince Higashikuni, the Emperor's uncle, heads the new cabinet formed in order to deal with the post-surrender situation.

September   Japan formally signs the surrender instruments and the Allied occupation of the country starts. General Douglas MacArthur, Supreme Commander for the Allied Powers (SCAP), establishes his headquarters in Tokyo.

October   Prince Higashikuni, faced with SCAP orders for a sweeping reform, yields premiership to Kijūro Shidehara.

November   New political parties are formed.

1946

January   The Emperor formally disclaims divinity.

February   Land reform program starts.
            SCAP orders purge of wartime leaders from public office.

April   The first postwar general elections are held and the conservatives gain the majority of votes; Shigeru Yoshida becomes Prime Minister.

May   International Military Tribunal for the Far East starts in Tokyo to try 28 major war criminals.

October   New Japanese Constitution, to replace the old Meiji Constitution, is promulgated.

1947

January   Scope of purge is extended to include lesser officials. Government workers' union plans a general strike but SCAP bans it.

68

March	Popular elections of prefectural governors take place. (Heretofore, the governors had been appointed by the central government.)
April	Nine-year compulsory education (6-year grade school and 3-year middle school) is started. The first general elections in accordance with the new Constitution are held and the Socialist Party emerges as the largest party in the lower house of the Diet.
May	The new Constitution becomes effective and the Socialist leader, Tetsu Katayama, heads a new coalition government.
December	Reform of police force is effected through new legislation.

1948

March	Hitoshi Ashida, conservative member in the coalition government, replaces Katayama as head of the cabinet.
September	Student strikes over increases in tuition; *Zengakuren* is organized.
October	Yoshida, for the second time, forms a cabinet after the coalition government collapses in the midst of a financial scandal involving cabinet ministers.
November	International Military Tribunal ends; seven, including former Premier Hideki Tōjō, are sentenced to death and executed.

1949

January	General elections are held and the conservatives gain a plurality; Yoshida remains in office.
February	New economic recovery plan adopted on urging of American economic experts, headed by Joseph Dodge.
April	New foreign exchange rate ($1 = ¥360) becomes official.
May	U.S. announces the termination of reparations removals, to aid Japanese economic recovery.

1950

January	The Japan Communist Party is criticized by the Cominform as too moderate (the Nosaka line) and a more militant policy is adopted.
May	A large anti-Government demonstration, sponsored by left-wing groups, takes place in Tokyo
June	SCAP bans public demonstrations; Communist leaders are purged; Korean war starts; SCAP orders creation of National Police Reserve.
September	SCAP orders purge of Communists from mass communications media.

| October | Prominent figures who had been purged at the beginning of the occupation are readmitted to public life. |

1951

January	The Socialist Party decides to favor neutralism in the Cold War and to oppose a peace treaty with one side only as well as the maintenance of foreign bases in Japan.
April	General MacArthur is replaced by General Matthew B. Ridgway as head of SCAP.
June	A large-scale rehabilitation of wartime leaders begins. Japan becomes a member of UNESCO.
September	International conference on Japanese Peace Treaty is held at San Francisco; the Peace Treaty is signed (U.S.S.R. and China, among others, are not signatories); simultaneously, the U.S.-Japan Security Pact is concluded.
October	The Socialist Party splits over the San Francisco treaties.

1952

January	South Korea announces establishment of the Rhee Line, excluding Japanese fishermen from waters adjacent to the peninsula.
February	The U.S.-Japan Administrative Agreement is signed, defining the status of U.S. forces in Japan.
March	Japan is permitted by the Allied Occupation authorities to manufacture military weapons.
April	Plants that had been designated for removal as part of reparations are returned to the Japanese; the ban on the use of *zaibatsu* trademarks is lifted.
	The peace Treaty becomes effective and Japan regains its sovereignty.
June	First unofficial trade agreement is signed between Japan and Communist China.
July	Japan signs a peace treaty with Nationalist China.
August	The Safety Agency is established to administer Japan's Safety Forces (formerly the National Police Reserve).
October	In the first general elections since Japan regained sovereignty, the conservatives retain control in the Diet and Shigeru Yoshida remains as premier.

1953

| April | The conservative government is increasingly challenged by internal dissenters and general elections are held; Yoshida and his party continue in power but Socialist votes increase. |

July	Negotiations start between Japan and the U.S. for a defense assistance agreement providing for U.S. military aid in equipment to Japan. An armistice is signed in Korea.
September	The U.S.-Japan Administrative Agreement is revised giving Japan jurisdiction over American servicemen off duty.
October	Second unofficial trade agreement is signed with mainland China.
December	The U.S. returns Amami Islands to Japan.

1954

March	Japanese fishermen become victims of U.S. atomic tests at Bikini and public agitation against nuclear tests gains momentum. Mutual Defense Assistance Agreement is signed between the U.S. and Japan to provide a practical basis for implementation of the 1951 Security Pact.
July	The Defense Agency replaces Safety Agency and Safety Forces are reorganized as Self-Defense Forces.
November	Ichirō Hatoyama spearheads opposition to Yoshida within the conservative ranks.
December	Yoshida, after six consecutive years in office, yields the post of Prime Minister to Hatoyama.

1955

February	Hatoyama remains as head of the Cabinet when his group gains victory in general elections.
May	Third unofficial Japan-Communist China trade agreement is concluded.
June	Negotiations with U.S.S.R. for normalization of diplomatic relations start.
October	The Socialist Party, split since 1951, reunites.
November	The conservative parties unite as the Liberal-Democratic Party.

1956

May	Japan-U.S.S.R. fishery agreement is signed.
July	National Defense Council is formed.
October	Japan-U.S.S.R. joint declaration on restoration of formal diplomatic relations is announced.
December	Japan is admitted to the United Nations. Tanzan Ishibashi replaces Hatoyama, who resigns as premier because of illness.

1957

February   Nobusuke Kishi succeeds ailing Ishibashi as Prime Minister.

June   Negotiations for revision of Japan-U.S. Security Pact begin.

1958

March   Fourth unofficial agreement on trade with Communist China is signed.

May   General elections; the conservatives win and Kishi keeps his cabinet.

June   Nagasaki flag incident; Communist China breaks off all trade relations.

1959

March   Public pressure begins to build up against proposed revision of the U.S.-Japan Security Pact.

April   Crown Prince Akihito is married to Michiko Shōda, a commoner.

August   Japan signs an agreement with North Korea on voluntary repatriation of Koreans from Japan.

November   Right-wing Socialists, led by Suehiro Nishio, split from the party over revision of the U.S.-Japan Security Pact.

1960

January   The new U.S.-Japan Security Pact is signed.

February   Socialist right-wing splinter group forms the Democratic-Socialist Party.

May-June   Public agitation against ratification of the new Security Pact reaches its peak in mass demonstrations around the Diet Building; the treaty is ratified by the Diet, but projected visit to Japan by President Eisenhower is cancelled.

July   Prime Minister Kishi resigns and is succeeded by Hayato Ikeda.

October   Socialist Party leader, Inejirō Asanuma, is assassinated by a right-wing youth.

November   General elections; the conservatives remain in power and Ikeda continues as premier.

1961

June   A cabinet-level joint committee on trade and economic matters is formed between the U.S. and Japan.

1962

January	A cabinet-level joint committee on cultural and educational affairs is organized between the U.S. and Japan.
June	The U.S. appoints first civil administrator of Okinawa. Un-
November	official trade agreement between Japan and Communist China is signed.

1963

February	A trade agreement is signed between Japan and U.S.S.R.
October	A Japanese industrial exposition is held in Peking.
November	General elections show continued gain by Socialists, but Liberal-Democrats win and Ikeda continues in power.

1964

January	Relations with the Republic of China strained for several months over Japan's decision to repatriate to the mainland Chou Hung-chin, a defector from Communist China.
April	Japan becomes a full member of the Organization for Economic Cooperation and Development (OECD).
May	Mikoyan visits Japan, but differences over the northern islands continue to hinder the signing of a peace treaty.
July	Ikeda is re-elected President of the ruling Liberal-Democratic Party, continuing as Premier with a re-assignment of Cabinet and Party posts.
October	Eighteenth Olympic Games held in Tokyo.
November	Eisaku Satō succeeds to premiership following Ikeda's resignation for health; cabinet continues unchanged. Sōka Gakkai founds the Clean Government Party (Kōmeitō).

1965

January	Satō visits President Johnson in Washington.
	Japanese Government approves export on private deferred-payment basis of a vinylon-manufacturing plant to mainland China, a test case in the government's China policy.
February	Japanese and South Korean Foreign Ministers sign Draft Treaty on Basic Relations.
	Japan opens trade office in Peking.
April	Japanese and South Korean officials sign agreements on outstanding issues concerning fishery, property claims and the legal status of Koreans in Japan.
May	Kōzō Sasaki, leader of radical wing of the Socialist Party, is elected Party Chairman, consolidating the Leftists' ascendancy in that party.

II. THE JAPANESE POLITY

A. *The Structure of Government*

The Constitution of Japan, promulgated in 1947, provides for three kinds of power: the sovereign power, which resides with the people, the symbolic power, which is exercised by the Emperor, and the governing power, which is held by the Diet, the Cabinet and other organs of the executive, and the Courts.

The People are sovereign. It is from their will that the Emperor derives his position and the central government, through their elected members of the Diet, its power. The people also have the power of review of appointments to the Supreme Court and of electing local officials. Their civil, economic and social rights are explicitly protected in the Constitution.

The Emperor is "the symbol of the State and the unity of the people," acting in their behalf to perform such ceremonial duties as appointing the Prime Minister and Chief Justice, promulgating the laws and treaties, convoking the Diet, etc. In all of these acts of state, he has no independent power of decision, but acts only with "the advice and approval of the Cabinet."

The Diet is "the highest organ of state power" and "the sole law-making organ of the State." It is composed of two chambers, the lower house called the House of Representatives and the upper, the House of Councillors; the lower house is the more powerful. Members of both houses are elected by popular vote. The terms of members of the lower house are fixed at four years but terminate ahead of schedule should the house be dissolved. The terms of members of the upper house are six years, half of the membership being elected every three years. The House of Councillors is not subject to dissolution. In addition to passing laws and ratifying

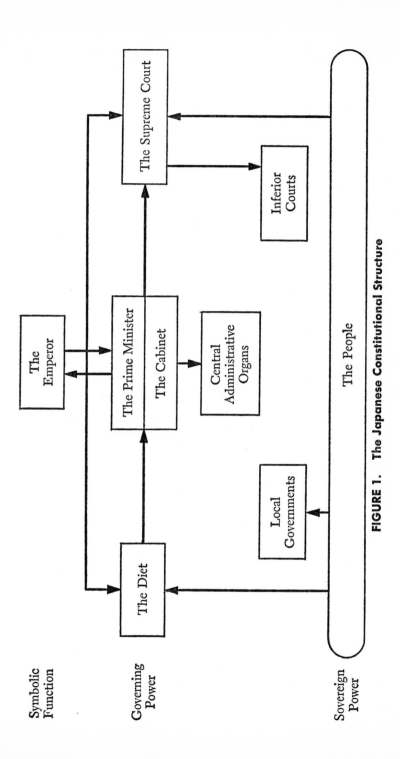

FIGURE 1. The Japanese Constitutional Structure

treaties, the Diet elects the Cabinet and supervises the executive. In case of serious conflict between the Diet and the Cabinet, either the Cabinet resigns or the Diet is dissolved by the Cabinet and new general elections take place.

The Cabinet is vested with the executive power and its head, the Prime Minister, is the head of the Japanese Government. The Prime Minister is designated from among the members of the Diet by a resolution (and then appointed by the Emperor); and he in turn appoints his own Cabinet. At present the membership of the Cabinet is 17. The law provides that a majority of the members should be chosen from among members of the Diet. The Cabinet, in exercise of executive power, is collectively responsible to the Diet.

The Supreme Court is the court of last resort with "power to determine the constitutionality of any law, order, regulation or official act." The Chief Justice of the Supreme Court is designated by the Cabinet and then appointed by the Emperor. The other 14 judges are appointed by the Cabinet, but are subject to popular review at the first House of Representatives elections following their appointment and every 10 years thereafter.

Inferior courts are established throughout the country. Judges are appointed by the Cabinet upon the nomination of the Supreme Court and act under the administration of the Supreme Court.

Central administrative organs, under the direction of the Cabinet, include Ministries in each major executive area, a number of Agencies, such as the Defense Agency, under the Prime Minister's Office, and relatively independent organs like the Board of Audit and Personnel Authority.

Local governments function in accordance with the autonomy principles. Japan is divided into 46 major administrative units (Tokyo Metropolis, the urban prefectures of Osaka and Kyoto, the island of Hokkaido, and 42 prefectures) and the assemblies and the heads of local governments are all elected by direct popular voting.

B. Political Parties

THE LIBERAL-DEMOCRATIC PARTY (Jiyū-Minshutō or commonly Jimintō)

By far the largest political party in Japan, with branches throughout the country, this conservative party and its predecessors have been in power since the end of World War II, except for a brief period (1947-1948). The present membership of the party is estimated at 1.5 million.

It started in 1945 as three separate parties, the Liberal, the Progressive and the Cooperative, which were essentially resuscitations of prewar political organizations. In the ensuing years these parties went through a series of splits and alliances but finally, in November 1955, merged into the present Liberal-Democratic Party.

THE SOCIALIST PARTY (Shakaitō)

The major opposition party in Japan today, the Socialist Party has been receiving support from about one-third of the electorate in recent general elections. The party was organized in 1945 by people who had belonged to various "left-wing" movements before the war. During the chaotic years immediately following Japan's surrender, the party achieved phenomenal growth, so much so that by 1947 the Socialists emerged as the largest group in the lower house of the Diet and Tetsu Katayama, the party leader, became Prime Minister. The Katayama regime, however, was not popular; and in the 1949 elections the Socialist power was drastically reduced. This debacle, together with the San Francisco Peace Treaty and Japan-U.S. Security Pact issues, brought about a split between the party's right-wing and its left-wing. The party was reunited in 1955 and remained so until 1960, when some of its right-wing group again split off to form the Democratic-Socialist Party.

THE DEMOCRATIC-SOCIALIST PARTY (Minshu-Shakaitō or commonly Minshatō)

Born early in 1960 in the midst of the sharp confrontation between right and left occasioned by the Security Pact issue, the party was composed of a splinter right-wing Socialist group led by Suehiro Nishio.

THE JAPAN COMMUNIST PARTY (Nihon Kyōsantō)

Originally founded in 1922, the Communist Party is the oldest political party now functioning in Japan. Although in the past its activities were frequently limited or suppressed over long periods of time, it is today a legal party. Postwar reorganization of the party was accomplished by veteran Communists coming out of jail or returning from exile. The party reached its zenith in 1949 when the Communist candidates won 10 per cent of the votes in general elections. In 1950, shortly before the Korean war, however, the leaders were purged from political life by the Occupation authorities and removed from positions in industry and communications media. It has only been since 1955 that the Communist Party has again begun to operate openly.

THE CLEAN GOVERNMENT PARTY (Kōmeitō)

The only religious party in Japanese history, the *Kōmeitō* was founded in November 1964, as the political arm of the Nichiren Buddhist organization *Sōka Gakkai*. The *Sōka Gakkai* began running candidates in the upper house elections in 1956, electing 3 in that year and 6 in 1959. These successes led it to organize the League, which, in 1962, boosted its representation in the upper house to 15, making it the third largest party group in that house. As the successor to the League, the Party has called for defense of the constitution and an "independent" foreign policy emphasizing ties with Asia.

A political group with representation only in the upper house of the Diet is:

THE SECOND HOUSE CLUB (Niin Kurabu)

For many years there were a considerable number of "independents" in the House of Councillors elections, who, once elected, usually organized themselves loosely into "negotiating groups" in order to strengthen their bargaining positions within the House. One of the more conservative of such groups, the Green Breeze Society, or *Ryokufūkai*, formed in 1947, wielded significant power until its membership was sharply decreased as a result of the 1959 elections. In 1960 the remaining members reorganized themselves as the *Dōshikai* and then, after the 1962 elections, as the Second House Club, which usually cooperates with the conservatives. It does not have a supporting party structure outside the Diet.

C. National Elections

Suffrage: All Japanese citizens over 20 years of age are qualified to vote, without regard to "race, creed, sex, social status, family origin, education, property or income." The percentage of eligible voters who cast ballots in general elections has run from a low of 60.93 percent in the 1947 upper house elections to a high of 76.99 percent in the 1958 lower house elections; but the postwar average is about 70 percent.

Procedure: For the House of Representatives elections the country is divided into 118 election districts, each sending from one to five members to the 467-member House. Each voter casts his ballot for only one candidate and the candidates receiving the highest number of votes win. For the 250-member House of Councillors there are two kinds of constituencies: 150 of the members are elected from prefectural constituencies (each prefecture is entitled to from 2 to 8 seats) and the remainder

TABLE 1. House of Representatives Election Results

(a) Number of seats won, by parties (figures in parenthesis indicate percentages).

Election Date	Democratic	National Cooperative	Liberal	Socialist / Right	Left	Labor-Farmer	Communist	Minor Parties	Independent	Total
April 25, 1947	121 (26.0)	29 (6.2)	131 (28.1)	143 (30.7)		7 (1.5)	4 (0.8)	25 (5.4)	13 (2.8)	466
Jan. 23, 1949	69 (14.8)	14 (3.0)	*Democratic-Liberal* 264 (56.7)	48 (10.3)		7 (1.5)	35 (7.5)	17 (3.6)	12 (2.6)	466
Oct. 1, 1952	*Reform* 85 (18.2)		*Liberal* 240 (51.4)	*Right* 57 (12.2)	*Left* 54 (11.6)	4 (0.9)	0 (0.0)	7 (1.5)	19 (4.1)	466
April 19, 1953	*Reform* 76 (16.3)	*Hatoyama* 35 (7.5)	*Yoshida* 199 (42.7)	66 (14.2)	72 (15.4)	5 (1.1)	1 (0.2)	1 (0.2)	11 (2.4)	466
Feb. 27, 1955		*Democratic* 185 (39.6)	*Liberal* 112 (24.0)	67 (14.3)	89 (19.1)	4 (0.9)	2 (0.4)	2 (0.4)	6 (1.3)	467
May 22, 1958			*Liberal-Democratic* 287 (61.5)	*Socialist* 166 (35.5)			1 (0.2)	1 (0.2)	12 (2.6)	467

SOURCE: *Japan Statistical Yearbook*, 1964, p. 896; 1963, p. 456; *Asahi Shimbun* (Morning Edition), November 23, 1963, pp. 1-2.

TABLE 1. House of Representatives Election Results (continued)

(a) Number of seats won, by parties (figures in parenthesis indicate percentages).

Election Date	Democratic	National Cooperative	Liberal	Democratic-Socialist	Socialist	Communist	Minor Parties	Independent	Total
Nov. 20, 1960			296 (63.4)	17 (3.7)	145 (31.0)	3 (0.6)	1 (0.2)	5 (1.1)	467
Nov. 21, 1963			283 (60.6)	23 (4.9)	144 (30.8)	5 (1.1)	0 (0.0)	12 (2.6)	467

(b) Number of votes received, by parties (figures in parenthesis indicate percentages). (Unit: 1,000)

Election Date	Democratic	National Cooperative	Liberal	Socialist		Labor-Farmer	Communist	Minor Parties	Independent
April 25, 1947	6,840 (25.0)	1,916 (7.0)	7,356 (26.9)	7,176 (26.2)			1,003 (3.7)	1,490 (5.4)	1,581 (5.8)
Jan. 23, 1949	4,798 (15.7)	1,042 (3.4)	Democratic-Liberal 13,420 (43.9)	Socialist 4,130 (13.5)		Labor-Farmer 607 (2.0)	2,985 (9.7)	1,603 (5.2)	2,008 (6.6)
Oct. 1, 1952	Reform 6,430 (18.2)		Liberal 16,938 (47.9)	Right 4,108 (11.6)	Left 3,399 (9.6)	261 (0.7)	897 (2.6)	949 (2.7)	2,355 (6.7)

		Hatoyama	Yoshida						
April 19, 1953	6,186 (17.9)	3,055 (8.8)	13,476 (39.0)	4,678 (13.5)	4,517 (13.1)	359 (1.0)	656 (1.9)	152 (0.4)	1,524 (4.4)
		Democratic	*Liberal*						
Feb. 27, 1955		13,536 (36.6)	9,850 (26.6)	5,130 (13.9)	5,683 (15.3)	358 (1.0)	733 (2.0)	497 (1.3)	1,229 (3.3)
	Liberal-Democratic			*Socialist*					
May 22, 1958	22,977 (57.8)			13,094 (32.9)			1,012 (2.6)	279 (0.7)	2,381 (6.0)
		Democratic-Socialist		*Socialist*					
Nov. 20, 1960	22,740 (57.6)	3,464 (8.8)		10,887 (27.6)			1,157 (2.9)	142 (0.4)	1,119 (2.8)
Nov. 21, 1963	22,424 (54.7)	3,023 (7.4)		11,907 (29.0)			1,647 (4.0)	50 (0.1)	1,956 (4.8)

SOURCE: *Japan Statistical Yearbook, 1964*, p. 896; 1963, p. 456; *Asahi Shimbun* (Morning Edition), November 23, 1963, pp. 1-2.

TABLE 2. House of Councillors Election Results

Number of seats won, by parties. (The upper figures refer to national constituency seats and the lower to perfectural constituency seats.)

Values shown as: national constituency / perfectural constituency. Italic labels are the party designation used for that election period.

Election Date	Democratic	National Cooperative	Liberal	Socialist	Labor-Farmer / Democratic-Socialists	Communist	Ryoku-Fūkai / Dōshikai	Others	Independent	Total
April 20, 1947	6 / 22	3 / 6	8 / 29	17 / 30		3 / 1		5 / 7	58 / 55	100 / 150
June 4, 1950	*National Democratic* 1 / 8		18 / 34	*Socialist* 15 / 21	*Labor-Farmer* 1 / 1	*Comm.* 2 / 0	*Ryoku-Fūkai* 6 / 3	*Others* 1 / 2	12 / 7	56 / 76
April 24, 1953	*Reform* 3 / 5		16 / 30	*Socialist* 11 / 17		0 / 0	8 / 8	0 / 1	15 / 14	53 / 75
July 8, 1956	*Liberal-Democratic* 19 / 42			21 / 28		1 / 1	5 / 0	1 / 0	5 / 4	52 / 75
June 2, 1959	22 / 49			17 / 21		1 / 0	4 / 2	1 / 0	7 / 3	52 / 75
July 1, 1962	21 / 48			15 / 22	*Democratic-Socialists* 3 / 1	2 / 1	*Dōshikai* 2 / 0	0 / 0	8 / 4	51 / 76

SOURCE: *Japan Statistical Yearbook, 1949, p. 896; 1963, p. 456.*

are elected by the nation at large. Each voter casts ballots for one candidate in the prefectural constituency and for one candidate in the national constituency. The candidates receiving most votes win.

Candidates: The ratio of number of candidates to contested Diet seats in postwar general elections has averaged about two to one. No party so far has nominated candidates for every seat at stake and only the Liberal-Democratic Party has nominated enough candidates to give it a mathematical possibility of winning a majority in the Diet.

TABLE 3. **Postwar Prime Ministers and Their Cabinets**

Prime Minister	Party Affiliation	Date of Appointment
Naruhiko Higashikuni	—	August 17, 1945
Kijūrō Shidehara	Progressive	October 9, 1945
Shigeru Yoshida (I)	Liberal	May 22, 1946
Tetsu Katayama	Socialist	May 24, 1947
Hitoshi Ashida	Democratic	March 10, 1948
Shigeru Yoshida (II)	Democratic-Liberal	October 15, 1948
Shigeru Yoshida (III)	Democratic-Liberal	February 16, 1949
Shigeru Yoshida (IV)	Liberal	October 30, 1952
Shigeru Yoshida (V)	Liberal	May 21, 1953
Ichirō Hatoyama (I)	Democratic	December 10, 1954
Ichirō Hatoyama (II)	Democratic	March 19, 1955
Ichirō Hatoyama (III)	Liberal-Democratic	November 22, 1955
Tanzan Ishibashi	Liberal-Democratic	December 23, 1956
Nobusuke Kishi (I)	Liberal-Democratic	February 25, 1957
Nobusuke Kishi (II)	Liberal-Democratic	June 13, 1958
Hayato Ikeda (I)	Liberal-Democratic	July 19, 1960
Hayato Ikeda (II)	Liberal-Democratic	December 8, 1960
Hayato Ikeda (III)	Liberal-Democratic	December 9, 1963
Hayato Ikeda (IV)	Liberal-Democratic	July 18, 1964
Eisaku Satō (I)	Liberal-Democratic	November 9, 1964

III. JAPANESE SOCIETY

A. Interest Groups

One of the most significant developments of the postwar years in Japan has been the vigorous growth of groups representing special interests. Some, of course, are non-political, but many have played an important role in Japan's political life, contributing funds, candidates or organizational support to political parties of their choice, or engaging in mass campaigns to influence the citizenry. The following are a few of the most important.

1. BUSINESS

Japanese business is highly organized into a hierarchy of associations, by industry, by region, and, finally, nation-wide. The five national federations listed below are the most important, each exercising considerable influence on the economic and political life of the country.

The Federation of Economic Organizations (Keizai Dantai Rengōkai commonly Keidanren)

The most powerful representative of business interests, *Keidanren*, organized in 1946, is composed of trade associations and their federations, as well as business firms and individual businessmen. With an elaborate committee structure it considers public policy in all fields related to the economy and works closely with political leaders, particularly the conservatives, and with government ministries and agencies.

The Japan Federation of Employers Associations (Nihon Keieisha Dantai Remmei, commonly Nikkeiren)

Organized in 1948 primarily for the purpose of formulating and supporting management's policies toward labor, *Nikkeiren* is organized along regional and industrial lines.

The Japan Chamber of Commerce and Industry (Nihon Shōkō Kaigisho, commonly Nisshō)

First organized in 1878 and then reorganized in 1945, the Chamber's chief concern is with medium and small, rather than large, enterprises. The central Chamber of Commerce and Industry and the local chambers promote business activities, supervise commercial organizations, engage in market research, and provide liaison between business and government agencies.

The Japan Committee for Economic Development (Keizai Dōyÿkai)

Formed in 1946 by a group of young business leaders who, in their individual capacities, were concerned for the future of capitalism in Japan, it is now organized along lines similar to the Committee for Economic Development in the United States and devotes itself to analysis of the national economy and of the role of business in society.

The Japan Foreign Trade Association (Nihon Bōekikai)

Organized in 1957 through a merger of four different organizations then engaged in encouraging Japanese trade abroad, the Association has been serving as the central organ representing trade enterprises vis-à-vis the government as well as the international business world.

2. LABOR

Over 7 million Japanese workers today belong to numerous labor unions throughout the country, most of which are organized by enterprises, rather than by crafts. Some of these unions remain independent while others affiliate with national unions. National unions, in turn, either remain independent or affiliate with each other in the giant federations listed below. At present, various national unions, with a total membership of about 1.5 million, are not associated with any national labor federations. While individual unions are mainly interested in wage and work conditions, the national federations seek in addition to advance labor's causes through political action.

General Council of Trade Unions of Japan (Sōhyō)

A giant organization, representing 60 affiliated national unions with a total membership of over 4 million, Sōhyō has been predominant in the Japanese labor movement since its establishment in 1950. Among its affiliates are such powerful unions as the Japan Teachers Union (Nikkyōsō) and the National Railway Workers Union (Kokurō). Marxist in ideological outlook, it is in agreement with the Socialist Party on a wide range of issues and has consistently supported that party in national elections and looked on it as its political instrument.

All-Japan Congress of Trade Unions (Dōmei Kaigi)

Formed in 1962 by the All Japan Trade Union Congress (Zenrō), the Japan General Federation of Labor Unions (Sōdōmei), and the All-Japan Conference of Government Workers Unions (Zenkankō), its organization represented an effort by more moderate, economic-minded labor federations to unite for economic and political action.

85

With 23 national unions as its affiliates and a total membership of a little over 1 million, it supports politically the Democratic-Socialist Party.

National Association of Industrial Unions (Shinsambetsu)

The smallest of the national centers of labor organizations, *Shinsambetsu* was formed originally in 1949 by a split in the *Sambetsu* organization, which had exercised great power in the early years of the Occupation. It has today 10 affiliates and a membership under 45,000, and tends to support the Socialist Party.

Liaison Conference of Independent Trade Unions (Chūritsu Rōren)

Unlike the preceding three, this is not a national federation but a loosely organized coordinating body created in 1956 by some of the independent unions. *Chūritsu Rōren*, now consisting of 18 national unions with a total membership of little over 1 million, remains "neutral" in politics and in controversy within the labor movement.

TABLE 4.   Labor Statistics

Year	Number of Trade Unions	Union Membership	Estimated Percentage of Workers Unionized
1955	30,012	6,166,348	39.8
1956	34,073	6,350,357	37.1
1957	36,084	6,606,275	37.1
1958	37,823	6,881,581	35.7
1959	39,303	7,077,510	33.3
1960	41,561	7,516,316	33.1
1961	45,096	8,154,176	35.4

SOURCE: *Mainichi Nenkan, 1963*, p. 304.

3. FARMERS

National Association of Agricultural Cooperatives (Nōkyō)

Established in localities throughout the country after the war, *Nōkyō* remains neutral on most political issues and acts primarily in matters related to credit, buying and selling farm products, storage, insurance, food processing and rural welfare.

All-Japan Federation of Farmers Unions (Zennichinō)

Organized in 1958 when the splinter groups of the Japan Farmers Unions (*Nichinō*) were reunited, *Zennichinō* embraces a wide range of farm groups of left-wing political orientation, from moderate Socialists to Communists. While energetic in advancing the farmers' interests, it is also very active politically. Consequently, when there was a split in the

Socialist Party in 1960, the right-wing Socialists in *Zennichinō* likewise left the organization to form the National Federation of Farmers (*Zennōdō*). There is a third organization called the National Farmers League (*Zennōren*), which is a small, politically "neutral" group.

4. WOMEN

Since 1945 there has been a marked increase in the number of women's organizations and women have been very active in various fields, including politics. (Today there are 23 women in the national Diet, 7 in the lower house and the rest in the upper house.) By far the largest among women's organizations is the Federation of Housewives (*Shufu Rengōkai*), established in 1948, which has sought to solve in practical ways various daily problems encountered by housewives. Although this is a national federation, its activities are largely urban-centered.

5. YOUTH

All-Japan Federation of Student Self-Governing Organizations (Zengakuren)

Originally organized in 1948 in connection with student strikes over tuition raises and other campus grievances, this federation later turned into a militant political action group. In it are represented student self-government organizations in various colleges and universities throughout the country. At a very early stage, the organization's leadership was taken over by students sympathetic to Communism, and the *Zengakuren* for years has been identified with the extreme left wing in Japanese politics. In 1960, the Federation was in the forefront of a movement opposing the new U.S.–Japan Security Pact. Since the failure of that effort, it has split into a number of factions and has, to a large extent, lost initiative to other youth organizations.

All-Japan Student Liaison Conference for Opposing the Security Pact and Defending Democracy (Heimin Gakuren)

Sponsored locally by the Japanese Communist Party, the *Heimin Gakuren* is the leading threat to the *Zengakuren* for the affiliation of Japan's student population.

Democratic Youth League (Minseidō)

Organized in 1956, *Minseidō* is the youth affiliate of the Japan Communist Party. It now numbers 80-100,000, recruiting largely among students and young laborers. It carries on vigorous cultural as well as political activities, and like the Japan Communist Party, supports the "Chinese line" in the Sino-Soviet dispute.

Socialist Youth League (Shaseidō)

Affiliated with the Socialist Party, the *Shaseidō* has a membership of about 30,000, consisting largely of young labor union activists. It has not pursued a very vigorous program and has had difficulty in achieving an identification distinct from that of its *Sōhyō* sponsors.

Youth Department of Sōka Gakkai

An affiliate of Japan's most militant and fastest growing religious sect, the Youth Department or *Seinenbu* of *Sōka Gakkai* today numbers more than 1 million members. Religious in orientation, it nevertheless has rather vaguely defined political interests and competes for members with other youth organizations, particularly among the poorer elements of the population.

Liberal Youth League (Jiseidō)

The youngest competitor for the political allegiance of Japan's youth, the *Jiseidō* was formed in 1963 as an affiliate of the ruling Liberal-Democratic Party. It aims to reach various hitherto non-political youth organizations and to give them a conservative political orientation.

6. RIGHT-WING EXTREMISTS

Following the end of the Allied Occupation in 1952, various right-wing groups began appearing in increasing numbers. Today, there are about 25 national organizations with a membership of about 20,000 and about 300 local groups with a membership of some 25,000. These have made considerable efforts to recruit youth and to win support from religious organizations so as to build up a right-wing organization with a wide base and appeal that could become a "third party" alternative to the Liberal-Democrats and the Socialists. One of the largest federations is the All-Japan Conference of Patriots' Organizations (*Zennihon Aikokusha Dantai Kaigi*), founded in 1959. It has 90 member organizations but so far appears to have had little influence.

Some right-wing extremists, singly or as groups, have resorted to acts of terrorism, some recent cases being the following:

July 1960: Prime Minister Nobusuke Kishi was wounded, in the wake of the U.S.-Japan Security Pact controversy.

October 1960: Inejirō Asanuma, Secretary-General of the Socialist Party, was assassinated while on an election campaign.

February 1961: The household of Hōji Shimanaka, publisher of *Chūō Kōron*, a national magazine, was attacked because of alleged lack of respect for the Emperor in one of the magazine's articles.

December 1961: A group of rightists was arrested for plotting the assassination of top government officials; the so-called *Sammu* case.

7. PEACE GROUPS

Japan Council Against Atomic and Hydrogen Bombs (Gensuikyō)

Organized in 1955, following the Bikini incident the previous year, *Gensuikyō*, largely leftist in leadership, has been the best organized and the most vociferous among peace groups in Japan. It has consistently criticized nuclear testings. Since 1961, however, the organization has been greatly weakened because of internal dissensions, largely along political party lines. In that year, the Democratic-Socialist Party group left *Gensuikyō* and set up a new body, which some Liberal-Democratic Party members also later joined. Then, in 1962, the Socialist-Communist dispute over the resumption of Soviet testing resulted in another serious breach within *Gensuikyō*, with the Socialist members splitting off to form a third anti-bomb organization.

8. RELIGIOUS GROUPS

Since the end of World War II a noteworthy development has been the growth of the so-called "new religions," generally eclectic faith healing sects drawing on Shinto, Buddhist and other religious traditions. Most have shown little or no interest in politics, the one exception being:

Value Creation Society (Sōka Gakkai)

Originally formed in 1930 as a lay movement within the Nichiren Buddhist organization, it has taken on new life in the years since the Occupation. Preaching the importance of beauty, goodness and value, it has adopted militantly aggressive methods to expand its membership, which now numbers 10 million. Attacking government corruption and expressing criticism of both democracy and Communism, it has become increasingly active in politics through its political auxiliary, the Political League for Public Enlightenment, and since November 1964, its own Clean Government Party.

9. VETERANS

After the Imperial Reservists' Association (*Teikoku Zaigō Gunjinkai*) was disbanded by the Occupation authorities, a series of organizations were set up by former servicemen for mutual help in matters ranging from pension payments to smooth transition to civilian life. Today there are two major organizations of this kind, the *Kaikōsha* (Army Club) and *Suikōkai* (Navy Club); both founded in 1952, they consist of graduates of former service academies and are primarily mutual aid societies.

As Japan's rearmament became an issue, however, the veterans started to organize themselves into political groups, the most significant among which is:

Japan Veterans League (Kyōyūren)

Organized in 1956 through a merger of various veterans' groups interested in rearmament, this nation-wide organization today has more than 1 million members, most of whom are former army and navy officers. With ex-generals and ex-admirals as its leaders, *Kyōyūren* is a highly conservative group politically, which favors Japan's rearmament.

B. Mass Communications Media

1. NEWSPAPERS

There are more than 150 newspapers in Japan and nearly 40 million copies are sold every day. Predominant are three major national papers which are widely distributed and account for almost half of the nation's total newspaper circulation. All three pride themselves on being politically independent.

Asahi Shimbun (published since 1879; daily circulation 6.8 million) The most widely read paper in Japan, the *Asahi* has been extremely influential over the years. Liberal in outlook, it has remained under the management of the Murayama family from the beginning.

Mainichi Shimbun (published since 1872; daily circulation 5.6 million) A popular, independent paper, thought to be a bit more conservative than the *Asahi*, it is known for its accurate and speedy reporting.

Yomiuri Shimbun (published since 1874; daily circulation 4.3 million) Flashier in style than the other two, this paper saw a phenomenal growth under the long management of Matsutarō Shōriki, whose family today is the paper's majority stockholder.

Smaller than the Big Three but of considerable influence in the financial and commercial fields are:

Nihon Keizai Shimbun (published since 1876; daily circulation 1.2 million) The most authoritative daily covering economic news, this is pre-eminently the businessman's newspaper. Although started by the Mitsui group, it is now published by a publicly owned corporation.

Sankei Shimbun (published since 1933; daily circulation 2.8 million) The youngest of the major presses, *Sankei* originally started in Osaka as *Nihon Kōgyō Shimbun.* The paper grew in size through two major mergers, in 1942 and then in 1959, which resulted in extending its domain to western Japan and eventually to the entire nation. (Although the present *Nihon Kōgyō Shimbun* shares its origin with *Sankei Shimbun*, the managements of these two papers are entirely separate and independent of each other.)

2. WIRE SERVICES

Kyōdō and *Jiji* are the two major news services, the former having a much wider network than the latter, both at home and abroad. They are successors to the *Dōmei*, the war-time wire service, which was disbanded by the Occupation authorities in 1945.

3. MAGAZINES

With a total circulation of over 1 billion a year, Japan enjoys the largest magazine sales in the world. Most popular are the major women's magazines, whereas the most influential are such monthlies as *Sekai*, *Chūō Kōron* and *Bungei Shunjū*, which, although limited in distribution, are widely read by the educated and thus play an important role in molding public opinion. Japan also publishes over 20,000 books a year; the number of copies printed reaches some 200 million.

4. RADIO AND TELEVISION

There are over 350 radio stations in Japan and the number of receiving sets in use is over 10 million. Although only 10 years old, the television industry has had a phenomenal growth and today five networks, with 150 stations, are broadcasting. The Japan Broadcasting Association (NHK) has long occupied the predominant position; recently, however, private companies are expanding at a rapid pace, particularly in television.

TABLE 5. Mass Communications Statistics

(a) Daily newspapers

Country	Year	Number of Papers	Estimated Circulation	Copies per 1,000 of Population
Japan	1961	157	39,139,000	416
France	1961	136	11,800,000	257
W. Germany	1962	433	17,431,00	306
U.S.S.R.	1961	457	39,355,000	181
United Kingdom	1962	112	26,200,000	490
United States	1962	1,760	59,848,000	321

TABLE 5. Mass Communications Statistics _(continued)_

(b) Books published (1962)

Country	Number of Titles	Remarks	
Japan	22,010	First editions:	12,293
France*	12,705		
W. Germany	21,481		
U.S.S.R.	43,367	Books placed on market only:	17,090
United Kingdom	25,079	First editions:	18,975
United States*	21,901	First editions:	14,238

* 1961.

(c) Radio broadcasting: receivers

Country	Number of Receivers	Remarks
Japan	18,651,000	Number of licenses issued.
France	13,776,000	Number of licenses issued.
W. Germany	16,696,000	Number of licenses issued.
U.S.S.R.*	44,000,000*	Number of licenses issued.
United Kingdom	15,580,000	Number of licenses issued.
United States †	183,800,000	Number of sets in use (estimate).

* 1960.
† 1961.

(d) Television broadcasting: receivers (1962)

Country	Number of Receivers	Remarks
Japan	12,612	Number of licenses issued.
France	3,427	Number of licenses issued.
W. Germany	7,213	Number of licenses issued.
U.S.S.R.	8,300	Number of licenses issued.
United Kingdom	12,231	Number of licenses issued.
United States	60,000	Number of sets in use (estimate).

SOURCE: UNESCO, in _U.N. Statistical Yearbook, 1963,_ pp. 667-686.

IV. JAPANESE PERSONALITIES

A. Political Party Leaders

THE LIBERAL-DEMOCRATIC PARTY

Aiichirō Fujiyama (1897-) A graduate of Keio University and veteran business executive with experience in the sugar refining and chemical industries, Fujiyama was at one time President of the Japan Chamber of Commerce and Industry. He became active politically in the postwar years and in 1957 was brought into the Kishi Cabinet as Foreign Minister. Although he lost out in the struggle for the Premiership in 1960 and 1964, he remains a leading contender for that post in the future.

Takeo Fukuda (1905-) Graduate of Tokyo University, he was a civil servant in the Ministry of Finance until 1950. He became active in politics in 1952 when he was elected to the Diet, and rapidly rose in the hierarchy of the Liberal-Democratic Party, eventually becoming the party's Secretary-General. In 1959, he joined the Kishi cabinet as Minister of Finance and has now taken over the leadership of one segment of the Kishi faction.

Hayato Ikeda (1889-) Prime Minister of Japan 1960–1964, Ikeda is a graduate of Kyoto University. He distinguished himself as a tax expert in the Finance Ministry, where he worked until 1948; he was then drawn to politics, winning a seat in the House of Representatives. He has since served in a number of conservative cabinets, either as Minister of Finance or Minister of International Trade and Industry. Exponent of an economic policy of growth, he is one of the architects of Japan's postwar prosperity.

Tanzan Ishibashi (1884-) Upon graduation from Waseda University, he became a newspaper reporter for the *Mainichi*, then moved to the *Tōyō Keizai Shimpō* (Japan Economist), where he became one of

Japan's chief economic publicists in the prewar period. In 1946 he was appointed Finance Minister in the Yoshida Cabinet, but was soon purged. Upon his return to politics in 1951 he allied with Hatoyama and Kishi, and in 1956 succeeded the ailing Hatoyama as Premier, only to yield to Kishi two months later because of illness. He is now in semi-retirement, but continues active in the cause of improving relations with Communist China.

Hakuei Ishida (1914-) A graduate of Waseda University, he is one of the youngest influential members of the ruling Liberal-Democratic Party. Having already held posts that include the Secretary-Generalship of the Cabinet and the Ministry of Labor, his star is expected to rise in the future.

Mitsujirō Ishii (1889-) An elder conservative politician, Ishii graduated from Hitotsubashi University and began his career as a civil servant in the Metropolitan Police and then in the colonial government on Taiwan. Later he turned to the *Asahi* newspaper, of which he became a Board member and to politics. He was one of the principal organizers of the Liberal Party in 1945 and its successor, the Liberal-Democratic Party, which he has served in many high posts. He has also held portfolios in the Yoshida and Kishi Cabinets, but has been disappointed in his efforts to attain the Premiership.

Shōjirō Kawashima (1890-) After graduation from Senshū University in Tokyo, he traveled widely in the United States; after returning home he joined the *Tokyō Nichinichi Shimbun* as a political reporter. Soon turning to politics, he served as secretary to the Mayor of Tokyo and eventually became Secretary-General of the prewar Seiyūkai Party. He joined the Liberal Party when it was organized after World War II and later served as the party's Secretary-General. In 1955 he was made Minister of State and rose by the summer of 1964 to become vice president of the Party.

Nobusuke Kishi (1896-) A graduate of Tokyo University, he distinguished himself in prewar days in the Ministry of Commerce, the administration of Manchukuo, and in Tōjō's Cabinet. Purged after the war, he returned to politics in 1952. Aided by his brother, Eisaku Satō, he allied first with Yoshida, then with Hatoyama, and finally helped to bring about the conservative merger in the Liberal-Democratic Party. He served as Foreign Minister under Ishibashi and in 1958 succeeded to the Premiership, which he held until driven from office in 1960 by the uproar surrounding the Security Pact ratification. He continues to be influential in the conservative movement.

Ichirō Kōno (1898-1965) One of the powerful faction leaders in the Liberal-Democratic Party, Kōno was a graduate of Waseda. After reporting for the *Asahi*, he soon turned to politics, winning a seat in the Diet in 1932. When the Liberal Party was organized in 1945, he played a key role, becoming its first Secretary-General. He was soon estranged from the party, however, and later joined forces with the Hatoyama group, eventually serving as Minister of Agriculture in the Hatoyama cabinet in 1954. In 1956, he successfully negotiated the fishery agreement with the U.S.S.R. After that he served in various Party and Cabinet posts, vigorously pushing his bid for the Premiership.

Takeo Miki (1907-   ) A graduate of Meiji and the American University, Miki turned first to private business. In 1937 he won election to the Diet as its youngest member and has since maintained a reputation for youthful vigor and imagination. In 1945 he organized his followers into a conservative National Cooperative Party, which he then took into mergers with various other groups, including eventually in 1955 the Liberal-Democratic Party, where he has held a number of posts and served in several Cabinets.

Yasuhiro Nakasone (1918-   ) Upon graduation from Tokyo University in 1941 he entered the Home Ministry. He became Supervisor of the Metropolitan Police Board, a post from which he retired to enter politics. His rise in the conservative ranks has been rapid despite his relative youth.

Eisaku Satō (1901-   ) A bureaucrat turned politician, Satō succeeded Ikeda as Prime Minister in 1964 and serves concurrently as President of the Liberal-Democratic Party. Upon graduation from Tokyo University, he entered the Ministry of Transportation and spent his entire civil service career in the Ministry, eventually becoming Vice-Minister. In 1948, he was persuaded by Yoshida to leave the bureaucracy, join the Liberal Party and enter politics. Soon he was made Secretary-General of the Yoshida cabinet and in 1949 was elected to the lower house of the Diet. Thereafter, he served in a series of top party posts and was appointed Cabinet Minister many times. He is the younger brother of former Premier Kishi.

Shigeru Yoshida (1878-   ) The leading figure in postwar Japanese politics, Yoshida headed conservative cabinets for a total of seven years. He was a prominent diplomat in prewar Japan, retired from public life during the war, and re-emerged in 1945 as Foreign Minister in the Shidehara Cabinet, and in 1946 as Premier. A staunch conservative, he set Japan on its postwar courses of alliance with America and concentration on economic growth. Forced to yield the Premiership to Hatoyama in 1954, he remained powerful behind the scenes for many years, but has now retired from active political life.

THE SOCIALIST PARTY

Saburō Eda (1907-   ) In 1930 he dropped out of a commercial college in order to take an active part in the farmers movement and was soon appointed a member of the Central Executive Committee of the National

Farmers Party and later was elected to the Okayama Prefecture Assembly. His political activities were brought to a temporary halt when he was arrested in connection with the Popular Front movement in 1938. When World War II ended, he returned home, joined the new Farmers Party, and was elected to the upper house of the Diet on a Socialist ticket. He is now a member of the House of Representatives. Once a member of the Central Executive Committee of the Left-wing Socialist Party, and later the Secretary-General of the united Socialist Party, he continues to play a key role in the party as head of its Organization Bureau.

Jōtarō Kawakami (1889-   ) Retired as Chairman in May 1965, Kawakami has been a lawyer, university professor and politician. His activities in the proletarian political movement date back to prewar years. A graduate of Tokyo University, he taught at various institutions but left the teaching profession when elected to the Diet in 1928. He continued to work with labor groups and eventually served as Chairman of the prewar Labor-Farmer Party. In 1945 he took part in organizing the Socialist Party and, as a leader of its right wing, has been one of the central figures in its intra-party struggles.

Tomomi Narita (1912-   ) Young for a Japanese political leader, Narita is currently Secretary-General of the Socialist Party. A graduate of Tokyo University, he worked for years in one of the Mitsui companies. His political career started only after the end of World War II, a fact that sets him apart from the older generation of Socialist leaders who had been the workhorses of the left-wing movement since the early 1920's. Returned to the Diet time and again, he quickly emerged as an articulate spokesman for the left and a champion of its "structural reform" line.

Kōzō Sasaki (1901-   ) A leader of the Left wing in the Socialist Party, he has been involved in the farmer and labor movement since graduation from Dōshisha University. He was made chief secretary of the All-Japan Farmers Union in 1931. After World War II, he joined the newly organized Socialist Party and was elected to the House of Representatives. Within the Party he is a rival to the Eda-Narita leadership and in May 1965 succeeded in winning election as Chairman of the Party, succeeding Kawakami.

Mosaburō Suzuki (1883-   ) A veteran Socialist leader, Suzuki has been the Chairman of the Socialist Party for many years but is today semi-retired and holds only the honorary position of Party Advisor. After graduating from Waseda, he joined the socialist movement and served as Secretary-General of the prewar Proletarian Mass Party. After the war he became a member of the newly organized Socialist Party and was elected its General Secretary in 1949, becoming its Chairman two years later. In intra-party struggles he was for a long time the indomitable leader of the left wing.

Hiroo Wada (1903-   ) A graduate of Tokyo University, he worked in the government Planning Board for many years. After World War II, he turned to politics and became Minister of Agriculture and Forestry in 1946, also serving as Director-General of the Economic Stabilization Board in the Yoshida cabinet. In 1949, he switched his party affiliation to the Socialists and quickly emerged as one of the top leaders associated first with the Party's left wing, then with the moderates. Today a Diet member, he also heads the International Bureau of the party, calling for a policy of "positive neutralism."

THE DEMOCRATIC-SOCIALIST PARTY

Tetsu Katayama (1887-   ) A veteran Christian labor leader, Katayama briefly served in 1947 as the only Socialist Prime Minister in Japan's history. In the Socialist debacle the following year, however, he lost both his own Diet seat and leadership of the party as well. He continued active in the right wing of the divided Socialist Party for a time but has now been appointed Supreme Advisor to the Democratic-Socialist Party. He retains, however, a relatively independent position and devotes himself largely to writing.

Suehiro Nishio (1891-   ) The leader of the Democratic-Socialist Party, Nishio has been identified with Japan's socialist movement for the last half century. He began as a worker in a Sumitomo steel mill, then turned to activity in the labor union and proletarian party movement. In 1945 he became a member of the Central Executive Committee of the Sōdōmei labor federation and Secretary-General of the newly organized Socialist Party. In 1947 he joined the Katayama Cabinet and served as Deputy Premier in the Ashida coalition government that followed. A right-wing Socialist, he broke with the united leadership in 1959 to form his own more moderate Democratic-Socialist Party.

THE JAPAN COMMUNIST PARTY

Kenji Miyamoto (1908-   ) Secretary-General of the Central Committee of the Japan Communist Party, Miyamoto was born into a poor shopkeeper's family, was active in the student and left-wing literary movement in his Tokyo University days, and joined the Communist Party in 1931. Imprisoned for his Party activities from 1933 until 1945, he was released following Japan's surrender to become an influential member of the Central Committee and Secretary-General since 1958. He is the chief architect of the present Party Constitution and works closely with the pro-Chinese leadership.

Sanzō Nosaka (1892-   ) Chairman of the Central Committee of the Japan Communist Party, Nosaka is a graduate of Keio University. He has been active in the Party since 1922, but fled to Moscow in 1928, where he served the Comintern, and to Yenan in 1940. Returning home in 1946 he helped to reorganize the Party and direct it along peaceful lines. He disappeared from view between 1950 and 1955, but re-emerged to become Secretary-General of the Party, and in 1958 its Chairman. He is reportedly the leader of the dominant pro-China faction. First elected to the lower house of the Diet in 1946, he is now a member of the upper house.

B. Business Leaders

Tadashi Adachi (1883-) Upon graduation from Hitotsubashi University, he joined the Mitsui Trading Co. and then transferred to the Ōji Paper Co., of which he became, in turn, director, managing director and president (1942-46). After World War II, he was purged and depurged. Eventually he became president of the Tokyo Metropolitan Chamber of Commerce and Industry and president of Radio Tokyo. Today president of the Japan Chamber of Commerce and Industry, he also serves as an officer of the Japan Committee for Economic Development and the Japan Industrial Club.

Heitarō Inagaki (1888-) A leading industrialist, he heads the Japan Foreign Trade Association. A graduate of Keio University, he worked, in turn, for Furukawa & Co., Fuji Electric Machinery Co. and *Jiji Shimpo*. Serving as director for a number of companies, he was president of the Yokohama Rubber Manufacturing Co. between 1942 and 1946. Turning to politics in 1947 by getting elected to the lower house of the Diet, he became Minister of International Trade and Industry in the Yoshida cabinet of 1949. Soon returning to foreign trade business, he has been active in promoting Japanese trade abroad.

Taizō Ishizaka (1886-) One of the top industrialists in Japan, Ishizaka is today President of the powerful Federation of Economic Organizations. He graduated from Tokyo University, and rose to the presidency of the Dai Ichi Life Insurance Company. Not purged after the war, he devoted his major energies to "Tōshiba" (the Tokyo Shibaura Electric Company), of which he became President in 1949 and is now Chairman of the Board.

Yoshizane Iwasa (1906-) One of Japan's leading bankers, Iwasa rose through the former Yasuda Bank and is now president of its successor, the Fuji Bank. A prominent director of the Japan Committee for Economic Development, he is increasingly active in the field of overseas development.

Kazutaka Kikawada (1899-) Long associated with the electrical power industry in eastern Japan, Kikawada has been President of the Tokyo Electric Power Co. since 1961. Executive Director of the Japan

Committee for Economic Development and an influential director of the Japan Federation of Employers Associations, he has provided leadership particularly in areas of new technology, for example, in the aeronautical and atomic energy fields.

Shigeo Mizuno (1899-) A Tokyo University graduate, Communist labor organizer in the 1920's, scholar and translator of French literature, Mizuno became a convert to capitalism. Rising in postwar Japan to head, among other enterprises, the Kokusaku Pulp Company, the Cultural Broadcasting Company and the conservative newspaper *Sankei Shimbun*, he has been a powerful leader in reshaping the social and political attitudes of Japanese businessmen.

Kōgorō Uemura (1894-) Upon graduation from Tokyo University, he joined the government service and worked in the Ministries of Agriculture and Forestry and of Commerce and Industry, eventually becoming deputy chief of the Planning Board. Purged and depurged after the war, he joined the business world and has since been prominent in various high positions including that of vice-president of the Federation of Economic Organizations.

C. Labor Leaders

SŌHYŌ

Akira Iwai (1922-) Today the second most important leader in the giant *Sōhyō* organization, he began his career as a locomotive hand on the National Railways when he finished primary school in 1937. After the war, he joined the Socialist Party and was also involved in organizing the railway workers. Elected an officer of the National Railway Workers Union, he was dismissed in 1954 from the National Railways for his strike activity. He subsequently devoted his energies to *Sōhyō* and was elected Secretary-General of that organization in 1955. Since then, together with Ōta, he has guided *Sōhyō* primarily in the direction of political action, supplanting and attempting to guide the Socialist Party.

Kaoru Ōta (1912-) Chairman of the powerful *Sōhyō*, he also heads the Synthetic Chemical Workers Union. A graduate of Osaka University, he joined the Ube Nitrogen Co. in 1938. After World War II, he became Chairman of the company's workers union and eventually rose to prominence in the *Sōhyō* organization, becoming vice-chairman in 1952 and its Chairman shortly thereafter.

Fumihiko Takaragi (1920-) President of the All-Japan Communications Workers Union (*Zentei*), a strong mainstay of *Sōhyō*, Takaragi is a professional labor organizer, who, without higher education, has risen to

99

leadership not only in his own union and *Sōhyō*, but also in the Socialist Party, where he backs the moderate "structural reformers."

DŌMEI KAIGI

Kumazō Nakaji (1905-) Chairman of the All-Japan Congress of Trade Unions (*Dōmei Kaigi*), he also heads the All-Japan Seamen's Union (*Kaiin*). After primary school he went to sea, becoming deck officer of ocean-going vessels. In 1928 he joined the Social Democratic Party, and in 1933 he was elected an officer of the New Japan Seamen's Union. After the war he not only attained leadership in his own union and in the *Dōmei Kaigi*, but, as an admirer of Suehiro Nishio, right-wing Socialist leader, he has given powerful support to the Democratic-Socialist Party.

Minoru Takita (1912-) Chairman of the *Zenrō* and one of the most important leaders in *Dōmei Kaigi*. Ever since he began work in the Nisshin Spinning and Weaving Co. in 1931 after finishing a professional high school, he has been engaged in labor union activities. After World War II, he organized and headed the vast National Alliance of Textile Workers Unions (*Zensen Dōmei*), of which he is still chairman. He was a member of the Japanese delegation to the organizational meeting of the ICFTU and thereafter traveled widely in Europe and the United States. A severe critic of the left-leaning *Sōhyō*, he was instrumental in forming both the *Zenrō* and later the *Dōmei Kaigi*.

Haruo Wada (1919-) The Chief of the Organization Department of the All-Japan Seamen's Union (*Kaiin*), Haruo Wada is a protégé of Kumazō Nakaji. Serving since 1960 as Secretary-General of *Zenrō*, he has been working actively to align the Congress with right-wing socialism and currently with the Democratic-Socialist Party.

V. THE JAPANESE ECONOMY

A. Sources

For statistics and information on the Japanese economy, the following serial publications in English are reliable and current. Unless otherwise indicated, the tables and figures in this section are drawn from them.

Japanese Government Serials:
Economic Survey of Japan (Tokyo: Economic Planning Agency)
Japan Statistical Yearbook (Tokyo: Office of the Prime Minister)
Japanese Economic Statistics (monthly) (Tokyo: Economic Planning Agency)
Japanese Industry (Tokyo: Foreign Capital Research Society)
Monthly Statistics of Japan (Tokyo: Office of the Prime Minister)
Quarterly Bulletin of Financial Statistics (Tokyo: Ministry of Finance)

United Nations Serials:
U.N. Demographic Yearbook (New York: Statistical Office of the United Nations)
Economic Survey of Asia and the Far East (New York: Economic Commission for Asia and the Far East, United Nations)
U.N. Statistical Yearbook (New York: Statistical Office of the United Nations)

B. Population

TABLE 6. Population Trends

Year	Population (estimate) (in thousands)	Increase Rate (per 1,000)
1945	72,200	49.9
1946	75,800	31.0
1947	78,101	24.4
1948	80,010	22.2
1949	81,780	17.4
1950	83,200	16.4
1951	84,600	15.0
1952	85,900	13.7
1953	87,000	12.1
1954	88,293	11.8
1955	89,290	10.0
1956	90,170	8.4
1957	90,920	9.2
1958	91,760	9.5
1959	92,640	8.4
1960	93,420	9.3
1961	94,280	9.5
1962	95,180	10.3
1963	96,160	10.7
1964	97,190	na

SOURCE: *Japan Statistical Yearbook,* 1955/56, p. 11; and *Monthly Statistics of Japan,* February 1965, p. 3.

TABLE 7. Increase Rate and Density of Population Compared

Country	Total Population (1962 mid-year estimate)	Annual Rate of Increase (1958–1962)	Density (Population per 1 km², 1962)
Japan	94,930	0.9	257
France	46,998*	1.2	86
West Germany	54,061	1.3	220
U.S.S.R.	221,465	1.7	10
U.K.	53,441	0.8	219
U.S.A.	186,656	1.6	20
North Korea	10,500†	2.3	87
South Korea	26,520	3.3	269

* Provisional.　　　　　　　　　† Unofficial estimate.

SOURCE: U.N. *Demographic Yearbook,* 1963, pp. 123–141.

C. Productivity

FIGURE 2.   Economic Recovery

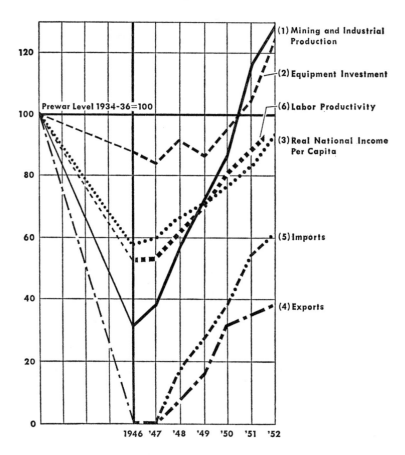

(Remarks) (1) Fiscal year. Source: Economic Planning Agency. (2), (3) Fiscal year. Economic Planning Agency. (4), (5) Calendar year. Ministry of Finance. (6) Fiscal year. Economic Planning Agency.

SOURCE: *Progress of the Long-term Credit Bank of Japan, Ltd.* (Tokyo: Long-term Credit Bank, 1963), p. 5.

103

TABLE 8. Economic Growth Rate (G.N.P.)
(Adjusted by 1934-36 Average Price)

	Real Gross National Product	
Fiscal Year	*1934–36=100*	*Increase over Previous Year*
		%
1946	65.0	—
1947	71.5	10.0
1948	83.2	16.4
1949	86.5	3.9
1950	97.0	12.2
1951	110.1	13.5
1952	121.7	10.5
1953	129.9	6.7
1954	134.2	3.3
1955	148.0	10.3
1956	161.3	9.0
1957	174.0	7.9
1958	179.6	3.2
1959	211.7	17.9
1960	239.6	13.2
1961	273.1	14.0
1962	284.6	4.2

NOTE: Figures for 1962 are of the Economic Plan.
SOURCE: Economic Planning Agency's White Paper on National Income, in *Japanese Industry, 1963*, p. 2.

TABLE 9. Principal Indicators under Government's Long-Term Economic Plan

	Base Year (A)	Final Year (B)	(B) (A)
	(1956–58 average)	*(1970)*	*(%)*
Total Population (in thousands)	91,110	102,220	112.2
G.N.P. (in 100 million yen in terms of prices in fiscal 1958)	97,437	260,000	266.8
National Income (ditto)	79,936	213,232	266.8
Per Capita National Income (in yen)	87,736	208,601	237.8
Personal Consumption Spending (in 100 million yen)	57,979	151,166	260.7
Gross National Capital Formation (ditto)	29,470	82,832	281.1
Mining and Manufacturing Production	100.0	431.7	431.7
Agriculture, Forestry, Fisheries Production	100.0	144.1	144.1
Employment (in thousands)	41,540	48,690	117.2
Exports (in million dollars)	2,687	8,485	315.8
Customs Base (ditto)	2,701	9,320	345.1
Imports (ditto)	2,549	8,080	317.0
Customs Base (ditto)	3,126	9,891	316.4

SOURCE: *Japanese Industry*, 1963, p. 6.

D. Foreign Trade

TABLE 10. Japanese Foreign Trade by Regions (in millions of U.S. dollars): Exports

Regions	1956	1957	1958	1959	1960	1961	1962	1963
Grand total	2,501	2,858	2,877	3,456	4,055	4,236	4,915	5,450
America:								
North America	621	670	769	1,164	1,226	1,187	1,537	1,646
U.S.A.	543	597	680	1,031	1,083	1,051	1,400	1,507
Latin America	171	157	205	238	298	341	343	346
Asia (non-Communist):								
East Asia	338	338	312	355	453	488	584	649
Southeast Asia	337	394	362	447	582	643	611	649
South Asia	193	237	200	186	271	255	270	309
Western Europe	246	317	327	365	480	548	695	726
Middle East*	107	159	157	179	185	213	206	244
Africa†	365	450	388	379	303	321	276	406
Oceania	44	58	80	102	182	138	180	223
Communist Countries‡	73	76	74	37	73	103	213	252
Mainland China	67	60	51	4	3	17	38	62
U.S.S.R.	1	9	18	23	60	65	149	158

* Including North Africa.
† Excluding North Africa.
‡ In Asia and Eastern Europe only.

SOURCE: Monthly Statistics of Japan, February 1965, pp. 47–64.

TABLE 11. Japanese Foreign Trade by Regions (in millions of U.S. dollars): Imports

Regions	1956	1957	1958	1959	1960	1961	1962	1963
Grand total	3,230	4,284	3,033	3,599	4,491	5,810	5,633	6,736
America:								
North America	1,211	1,793	1,179	1,269	1,757	2,363	2,064	2,396
U.S.A.	1,064	1,618	1,054	1,113	1,545	2,079	1,809	2,077
Latin America	351	311	259	328	310	481	477	564
Asia (non-Communist):								
East Asia	97	124	113	118	131	147	150	243
Southeast Asia	418	451	333	466	601	627	641	728
South Asia	218	214	144	162	184	200	176	239
Western Europe	223	385	262	350	397	559	606	674
Middle East*	273	391	349	387	451	542	611	797
Africa†	48	64	46	96	129	140	188	224
Oceania	286	437	260	339	404	531	493	596
Communist Countries‡	102	110	86	63	125	220	227	275
Mainland China	84	80	54	19	21	31	54	83
U.S.S.R.	3	12	22	39	87	145	149	162

* Including North Africa.
† Excluding North Africa.
‡ In Asia and Europe only.

SOURCE: *Monthly Statistics of Japan*, February 1965, pp. 47–64.

E. Employment

TABLE 12. The Labor Force (in thousands of people)

Year	Labor Force (A)	Employed	Wholly Unemployed (B)	Percent. of Unemployment (B)/(A) × 100
1954	40,550	38,890	670	1.7
1955	41,940	41,190	760	1.8
1956	42,680	41,970	710	1.7
1957	43,630	43,030	590	1.4
1958	43,870	43,240	630	1.4
1959	44,330	43,680	650	1.5
1960	45,110	44,610	500	1.1
1961	45,620	45,180	440	1.0
1962	46,140	45,740	400	0.9
1963	46,520	46,130	400	0.9

SOURCE: Bureau of Statistics, Office of the Prime Minister, in *Monthly Statistics of Japan*, June 1964, p. 7.

TABLE 13. Trends of Employment by Industrial Branches (in percentages)

End of	Total	Agriculture, Forestry	Fisheries	Mining	Construc- tion	Manufac- turing	Whole- sale, Retail, Banking, Insurance	Public Utilities	Services	Public Offices
1953	100.0	37.4	1.4	1.4	5.0	19.3	16.8	4.8	10.9	3.1
1954	100.0	34.7	1.5	1.8	4.3	19.5	19.2	4.7	11.0	3.3
1955	100.0	34.3	1.3	1.2	5.2	20.3	17.8	5.1	12.1	2.6
1956	100.0	32.1	1.4	1.4	4.8	20.1	19.1	5.2	13.1	3.0
1957	100.0	32.4	1.3	1.2	4.7	22.0	18.1	5.3	12.4	2.7
1958	100.0	30.0	1.1	1.3	5.6	21.4	9.5	5.4	12.7	3.0
1959	100.0	28.4	1.4	1.3	5.3	21.7	20.0	5.8	12.9	3.0
1960	100.0	27.0	1.5	1.1	6.3	21.7	20.0	5.4	13.6	3.0
1961	100.0	25.7	1.5	1.2	6.3	23.6	19.6	5.9	12.8	3.2
1962	100.0	25.8	1.5	1.1	6.5	23.4	20.0	6.0	12.3	3.3

SOURCE: Prime Minister's Office, *Japanese Industry*, 1963, p. 13.

VI. THE JAPANESE DEFENSE FORCE

A. Strength

Japan's military forces, disbanded by order of the Occupation authorities in 1945, have been rebuilt gradually in three stages: in 1950 a small National Police Reserve (*Keisatsu yobitai*) was authorized in order to maintain internal order; in 1952, after sovereignty was regained, this force was expanded and reorganized as the Safety Force (*Hoantai*); and in 1954 transformed into the present Self-Defense Force (*Jieitai*). Its authorized strength has grown as indicated in Table 14.

TABLE 14. Authorized Strength of Japan's Self-Defense Forces

Year	Ground	Maritime	Air	Staff	Total
1950	75,000				75,000
1951	75,000				75,000
1952	110,000	10,323			120,323
1953	110,000	10,323			120,323
1954	130,000	15,803	6,287	20	152,110
1955	150,000	19,391	10,346	32	179,769
1956	160,000	22,716	14,454	32	197,182
1957	160,000	24,146	19,925	34	204,105
1958	170,000	25,441	26,625	36	222,102
1959	170,000	27,667	33,225	43	230,935
1960	170,000	27,667	33,225	43	230,935
1961	171,500	32,097	38,337	75	243,923
1962	171,500	33,292	39,058	75	243,923
Actual strength (1962)	144,892	32,208	36,122	75	213,297

NOTE: Figures include Police Reserve, Maritime *Keibitai*, etc., as well as SDF (civilian employees not included).

SOURCE: Authorized strength in *Bōei Nenkan* (also: Bōei Bōei sangyō kyōhai), 1960, p. 199; 1961, p. 201; 1963, p. 184. Actual strength in *Asahi Nenkan*, 1963, p. 315.

The Ground SDF consists of 13 divisions (actual strength today, 145,000 men); the Maritime SDF has 469 vessels with a total tonnage of 128,000; and the Air SDF has 1,100 planes.

B. Expenditures

Most of the modern military equipment and about one-third of its military expenses have been supplied to Japan by the United States in accordance with the Mutual Defense Assistance Agreement signed in 1954 and other understandings. Japan's own expenditures for defense have been rising, but remain relatively small.

TABLE 15. Japan's Defense-Related Expenditures

	Defense-Related Expenditures (in 100 mil. yen)	Index	Per Cent of Nat'l Budget	Per Cent of Nat'l Income
1953	1,231	100.0	12.0	2.1
1954	1,327	107.7	13.3	2.2
1955	1,327	107.7	13.1	2.0
1956	1,431	116.2	13.1	1.9
1957	1,436	116.7	12.1	1.7
1958	1,485	120.6	11.1	1.7
1959	1,556	126.4	10.3	1.6
1960	1,600	130.0	9.1	1.3
1961	1,835	149.1	8.7	1.3
1962	2,137	173.6	8.6	1.4
1963	2,412	195.9	8.5	1.4

SOURCE: *Bōei Nenkan*, 1961, p. 291, for 1953-55 data; *Bōei Nenkan*, 1963, p. 264, for 1956-63 data.

C. Control

Civilian supremacy has been established over the Self-Defense Forces by placing them under the command of the Premier, who acts with the advice of a National Defense Council consisting of relevant Cabinet ministers, through a Defense Agency, headed by a civilian Director with a civilian Secretariat.

FIGURE 3. The Self-Defense Establishment

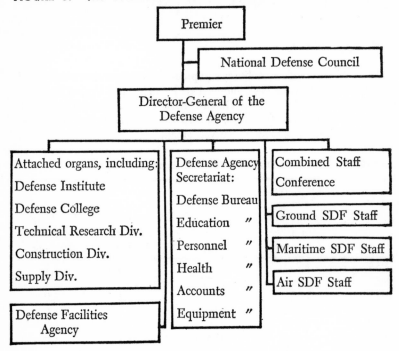

D. *The United States-Japan Mutual Defense Arrangements*

In addition to the Mutual Defense Assistance Agreement of 1954 under which the United States has been contributing substantially to the rearmament of Japan, the United States has been sharing direct responsibility for the defense of Japan under the Treaty of Mutual Cooperation and Security, signed in Washington on January 19, 1960, as a revision of the original Security Pact of 1951. The central military clauses of the 1960 Treaty are as follows:

Article III. The Parties, individually and in cooperation with each other, by means of continuous and effective self-help and mutual aid will maintain and develop, subject to their constitutional provisions, their capacities to resist armed attack.

Article IV. The parties will consult together from time to time regarding the implementation of this Treaty, and, at the request of either

112

Party, whenever the security of Japan or international peace and security in the Far East is threatened.

Article V. Each Party recognizes that an armed attack against either Party in the territories under the administration of Japan would be dangerous to its own peace and safety and declares that it would act to meet the common danger in accordance with its constitutional provisions and processes.

Any such armed attack and all measures taken as a result thereof shall be immediately reported to the Security Council of the United Nations in accordance with the provisions of Article 51 of the Charter. Such measures shall be terminated when the Security Council has taken the measures necessary to restore and maintain international peace and security.

Article VI. For the purpose of contributing to the security of Japan and the maintenance of international peace and security in the Far East, the United States of America is granted the use by its land, air and naval forces of facilities and areas in Japan.

Originally very substantial, the American forces stationed in Japan had been reduced by 1964 to about 6,000 Army, 14,000 Navy and 25,000 Air Force, excluding forces on Okinawa.

I. CHRONOLOGY OF KEY EVENTS

1945

August   Korea liberated. U.S. forces occupy South Korea while Russian forces occupy North Korea.

December   Three-Power Foreign Ministers' conference in Moscow agrees on trusteeship for Korea.

1946

January   The Communists support the Moscow decision while other Korean political groups voice strong opposition to trusteeship. Meanwhile, U.S.–U.S.S.R. joint commission is set up in pursuance of the Moscow agreement.

1947

October   The U.S.–U.S.S.R. Joint Commission adjourns without reaching an agreement. The U.S. presents the Korean question to the United Nations General Assembly. The United Nations decides on establishment of a unified Korean government through general elections and eventual withdrawal of foreign troops from the country. UN Commission on Korea is organized to supervise the projected elections.

1948

May   General elections are held in South Korea under UN supervision. North Korea bars entry of UN commission.

July   National Assembly of South Korea convenes, adopts a constitution and elects Syngman Rhee President of the Republic of Korea.

August	Republic of Korea comes into existence on the third anniversary of the nation's liberation.
September	Democratic People's Republic of Korea is organized in North Korea. Kim Il-sŏng is elected Premier.
December	U.S.S.R. announces withdrawal of its troops from North Korea.

1949

January	The U.S. formally recognizes South Korea.
March	Soviet Union and North Korea sign an agreement on economic and cultural cooperation.
June	American forces are withdrawn from South Korea.
October	The Chinese Communist government is organized in Peking and a formal diplomatic relationship is established with North Korea in the following month.

1950

January	A Mutual Security Assistance Agreement is signed between South Korea and the United States.
May	General elections in South Korea. The government party suffers a defeat.
June	Korean war starts. UN Security Council demands withdrawal of North Korean troops north of the 38th parallel. The same body approves military assistance to South Korea and U.S. forces are sent to Korea. North Korean forces occupy Seoul, capital of South Korea.
July	United Nations Command is established to conduct UN military action in Korea.
September	UN forces land at Inchon; North Korean troops retreat.
October	UN forces cross the 38th parallel and fight their way toward the Chinese border. P'yŏngyang, the North Korean capital, is occupied. Chinese volunteers enter Korea.
November	The UN forces start evacuation from North Korea.

1951

February	UN brands Communist China an aggressor.
June	The Russian delegate at the UN proposes cessation of hostilities in Korea.
July	Armistice talks start at Kaesŏng.
September	Japanese Peace Treaty is signed at San Francisco.
October	Armistice talks continue at Panmunjom.

1952

January	South Korea proclaims "the peace line." Japanese fishing in waters adjacent to Korea is prohibited.

February	A first round of talks between South Korea and Japan is held.
August	Rhee is re-elected as President after a fierce political fight with the opposition.
December	General Dwight Eisenhower, the President-elect of the U.S., visits the Korean front.

1953

April	The second round of talks between Korea and Japan.
June	An agreement on exchange of prisoners of war is signed at Panmunjom. South Korea opposes the agreement and releases 25,000 anti-Communist prisoners.
July	An armistice agreement is signed between the UN and Communist representatives.
August	U.S.–Korea Mutual Security Pact is initialed. (Formal signing takes place in Washington in October.)
September	U.S.S.R. and North Korea sign an economic assistance agreement for reconstruction.
October	The third set of Korean–Japanese talks are held.
November	An agreement is signed between Communist China and North Korea on economic and cultural cooperation.

1954

| April | Geneva Conference on Korean and Indo-Chinese questions is convened. In June the conference adjourns without reaching an agreement on Korea. |
| May | General elections in South Korea. |

1955

| December | North Korea announces death sentence for Pak Hŏn-yŏng, former Foreign Minister. |

1956

April	North Korea announces a new five-year plan.
May	Rhee is elected President for the third time, but Chang Myŏn of the opposition party is elected Vice-President.
August	Purge of high government officials in North Korea.

1958

April	Japan–Korea talks are resumed.
May	General elections in South Korea; the opposition party gains.
October	China announces withdrawal of volunteers from North Korea.

1959

August   North Korea and Japan agree on voluntary repatriation of Korean residents in Japan to North Korea.

1960

March   Rhee is elected President for the fourth time.

April   Public demonstrations against the government spread in South Korea; Rhee resigns as President and Hŏ Chŏng becomes Acting President.

June   South Korean National Assembly adopts a new Constitution providing for a parliamentary system; President Eisenhower visits Seoul.

July   General elections in South Korea; the Democratic Party emerges as the majority party.

August   Yun Po-sŏn is elected president of South Korea; Chang Myŏn becomes Premier.

October   The fifth Korean–Japanese talks are held.

November   North Korea proposes formation of a federation between North and South Korea.

1961

May   Military coup in South Korea; the Chang government is overthrown and the Constitution is suspended.

July   North Korea signs a Treaty of Friendship and Mutual Cooperation with the Soviet Union. A similar treaty is signed with Communist China.

September   North Korea announces seven-year economic plan.

October   The sixth talks between Korea and Japan open.

1962

January   South Korea announces five-year economic plan.

March   President Yun resigns and Gen. Park Chung-hee, Chairman of the military junta, becomes Acting President.

December   A new Constitution is approved in a national referendum in South Korea; it provides for a strong presidential system.

1963

January   New political parties are formed in Seoul in preparation for return to civilian government under the new Constitution.

October   Gen. Park is elected President of South Korea.

November   General elections in South Korea; Gen. Park's party wins victory.

December	Rule by military junta ends and civilian government takes over in Seoul.

1964

March	Widespread student demonstrations begin, at first opposing the Government's stand in the Japan–Korea negotiations, finally calling for the resignation of the Park leadership.
April	Negotiations with Japan are discontinued.
May	Resignation of the Premier and his Cabinet.
June	Martial law proclaimed in Seoul: Kim Chong-p'il resigns chairmanship of ruling Liberal-Republican Party and leaves the country.

1965

January	ROK announces decision to send troops to aid South Vietnamese.
February	Foreign Ministers of South Korea and Japan sign Draft Treaty on Basic Relations.
April	ROK and Japanese officials agree on outstanding issues concerning fishery, property claims and the legal status of Koreans in Japan.
	Opposition parties and students demonstrate in cities in opposition to government and its effort at rapproachement with Japan; riots quelled by the Army.
May	Numerous arrests of military and civilian leaders on charges of plotting to overthrow the government.
	Park visits Washington.

II. THE REPUBLIC OF KOREA (ROK)

A. Governmental Structure

The Constitution: The Republic of Korea came into being in August 1948, following a general election in South Korea under UN supervision. The Constitution of 1948 was subsequently amended several times, the most important change being the introduction in 1960 of a parliamentary government in place of a presidential system. The Constitution was suspended in 1961 by the military junta and the present Constitution was approved in a national referendum in 1962.

The President is the powerful head of state, appointing all administrative officials, including the cabinet. He exercises supreme command over the armed forces, has exclusive charge of foreign relations, and a limited veto power over legislation. He is elected by popular vote for a four-year term. Gen. Park Chung-hee was elected in October 1963.

The State Council, of which the President is Chairman, assists the chief executive in administrative affairs. The Prime Minister, who serves as Vice-Chairman of the Council, is appointed by the President, and, in turn, recommends to the President individuals for appointment to the other ministerial posts of the Council. Council members serve virtually at the President's pleasure since the Assembly may recommend their removal from office, but cannot require it.

The National Assembly is a unicameral national legislature. Its members are elected for a four-year term, which runs concurrently with that of the President. The Constitution fixes the number of deputies at "no less than 150 and no more than 200." At present the number is 175.

No independents are allowed to run for Assembly seats, every candidate being required by law to be nominated by a political party. It is also provided that an Assembly member cannot change his party affiliation during his term of office. He must resign from the Assembly if he wants to join a new party.

The Supreme Court is the highest court of the state. The justices are appointed by the President upon the recommendation of an independent Justice Recommendation Council. The Chief Justice's appointment requires Assembly approval.

B. Political Parties

The Democratic Republican Party (Minju Konghwa-dang) is the ruling party, having been successful both in the presidential and Assembly elections late in 1963. The party was organized under the sponsorship of the military junta as a nation-wide political organization to push ahead the junta's policies after introduction of a new constitutional government. Party membership, therefore, is made up of active supporters of the junta, most of whom have had comparatively little connection with the political parties of earlier days. The party is in favor of a strong presidential system, which alone, it believes, can bring political stability to the country and thereby hasten economic development.

In the general elections of November 1963, the opposition was divided among eleven different parties. Most of them are small groups, but efforts to unite them have failed. At present only four of them are represented in the National Assembly. They are as follows:

The Civil Rule Party (Minjŏng-dang), largest of the current opposition parties, is led by former president Yun Po-sŏn, and is made up largely of politicians loyal to him and active in the period before the military coup.

The Democratic Party (Minju-dang), second largest opposition party, is composed of former colleagues of Chang Myŏn, Premier at the time of the military revolution. Although technically a new party, this group has worked together since 1945, when it formed the Korean Democratic Party. Later variously called the Democratic-Nationalist Party and then the Democratic Party, it was the major opposition group during the long tenure of Syngman Rhee in the presidency.

The Party of the People (Kungmin-ŭi-dang) is likewise a small party of civilian politicians active since before the military coup. They form a faction loyal to former acting president Hŏh Chŏng.

The Liberal Democratic Party (Chayu Minju-dang) differs from the other three in being an opposition party made up not of civilian politicians so much as former military junta supporters at odds with the ruling group.

120

TABLE 16. Major ROK Political Parties

	Communists (underground and abroad)	Left-wing groups (underground and abroad)		"Provisional Government" (in exile in Nationalist China)	Syngman Rhee (in exile in the United States)
Japanese rule 1945	Communist Party	People's Party	Korean Democratic Party	Korean Independence Party	Independence Promotion Assn.
U.S. military occupation	1946 Workers' Party (South Korea) (Outlawed in 1948)	1946 Working People's Party (Disbanded in 1950)			
1948					
1949			1949 Democratic-Nationalist Party		1949 Korean Nationalist Party
1952					1952 Liberal Party
1955			1955 Democratic Party		
1956		1956 Progressive Party (Outlawed in 1958)			
1961 Military rule	Military junta — (All political parties suspended)				
1963	Democratic-Republican	Liberal-Democratic	Democratic Party	Civil Rule Party · Party of the People	Liberal Party

TABLE 17. ROK Presidential Elections

Accession to Office	Name (Party Affiliation)	Election Date	Votes Received	Total Votes Cast in the Elections
August 1948	Syngman Rhee (Independence Promotion Assn.)	July 20, 1948	180	196**
August 1952	Syngman Rhee (Liberal)	August 5, 1952	5,238,769	7,275,883
August 1956	Syngman Rhee	May 15, 1956	5,046,437	9,606,870
May 1960- August 1960	Syngman Rhee** Hŏ Chŏng (acting)	March 15, 1960	9,633,376	10,862,272
August 1960	Yun Po-sŏn* (Democratic)	August 12, 1960	208	259
March 1962	Park Chung-hee (acting)	—	—	—
December 1963	Park Chung-hee (Democratic-Republican)	October 15, 1963	4,702,640	11,036,175

* Elected but did not serve.
** Election by the National Assembly.

SOURCE: *Segye Yŏn'gam, 1959* (Seoul: Segye T'ongsin Sa, 1959), pp. 562-574; *Haptong Yŏn'gam, 1961* (Seoul: Haptong T'ongein Sa, 1961), pp. 549-550; *Korean Report,* Oct-Nov. 1963, p. 3.

TABLE 18. ROK National Assembly Elections

Election Dates	Total	Independence Pro-motion Association	Korean Democratic Party		Independents	Other Parties
May 10, 1948	198	53	29		85	31
		Korean Nationalist Party	*Democratic-Nationalist Party*			
May 30, 1950	210	24	23		127	36
		Liberal Party				
			Democratic Party			
May 20,1954	203	114	15		67	7
May 2, 1958	233	126	79		27	1
July 29, 1960	233	2	175		49	7
		Democratic-Republican	*Liberal-Democratic*	*Democratic*	*Civil Rule Party*	*Party of the People*
November 26, 1963	175	110	9	13	41	2

SOURCE: *Segye Yŏn'gam 1959*, pp. 566–567; *Haptong Yŏngam, 1961*, pp. 550–53; *Korean Report*, Oct.-Nov. 1963, p. 3.

C. Principal Personalities

Chang Myŏn (1899-) Former Prime Minister but now barred from political activities by the government. A leading Catholic layman, he is a graduate of Manhattan College in New York and for a long time headed a Seoul business school. Turning to politics after 1945, he was elected to the National Assembly and eventually served as Ambassador to the United States and then as Prime Minister under President Rhee. In 1952 he became a leader of the opposition Democratic Party and in 1956 was the party's successful candidate for the Vice-presidency. In 1960 he was defeated for re-election, but, following the downfall of the Rhee regime in the same year, was elected by the National Assembly to be Prime Minister. Less than a year later, his own government was ousted by the military junta.

Hŏ Chŏng (1896-) A leader of the Party of the People, he served as acting President for three months following the resignation of President Rhee in 1960. A graduate of Korea University in Seoul, he spent a number of years in exile (in France and the United States) during the Japanese rule of Korea. Since 1948 he has been active in politics and served as Minister of Social Affairs in 1950 and for a while as acting Prime Minister in 1951.

Park Chung-hee (1917-) Elected President in December 1963, he was educated at the Japanese Military Academy and was a professional soldier all his life until he resigned from the military service in 1963 in order to run for president. After serving in various posts in the South Korean Army, he led the military revolution in 1961.

Syngman Rhee (1875-1965) Former president, who resigned from office in 1960 and then lived in Hawaii. Educated in the United States, he was the foremost leader in the nationalist movement during the era of Japanese rule in Korea. For a time, he served as President of the Korean Provisional Government-in-exile. Returning home in 1945, he persistently agitated for immediate independence for Korea and was elected President when the Republic of Korea was established in 1948. Reelected to the presidency three times thereafter, he was the chief executive for twelve consecutive years until driven from office by student demonstrations in 1960.

Yun Po-sŏn (1897-) Former President, he is now a member of the National Assembly and leader of the opposition Civil Rule Party. He was a graduate of Edinburgh University, became Mayor of Seoul, and once served as Minister of Commerce and Industry under President Rhee. A power in the old Democratic Party, he was elected President of the Republic in 1960 and remained in office even after the military revolution of 1961, resigning only in March 1962.

124

Kim Chong-p'il (1926-) Nephew by marriage of President Park, Kim has been a storm center of power since, as a lieutenant colonel, he helped plan the Park coup in 1961. Promoted to colonel, he served the military regime as head of the potent Central Intelligence Agency. In preparation for the restoration of civilian rule in 1963, he organized and was chairman for the new Democratic Republican Party, which backed the President, and thereafter actively promoted the rapproachement with Japan. Anti-government riots in June 1964 forced his resignation and temporary "exile," but he returned that winter to resume activity behind the scenes.

D. Mass Communications Media

Some 45 daily papers are published in South Korea, with a total circulation of nearly two million. Among the more widely read papers, all published in the capital city of Seoul, are the following:

Hanguk Shinmun, started in 1949, a popular, independent daily that has experienced a rapid growth in the last decade.

Kyŏnghyang Shinmun, a respected Catholic paper since 1946, that was occasionally suspended because of its criticism of the government during the presidency of Syngman Rhee.

Seoul Shinmun, a government-sponsored paper.

Chosŏn Ilbo, an old paper (published since the 1920's) which has doggedly maintained its independent character through decades of political storms.

Tong-A Ilbo, the most colorful and controversial paper in the country, as well as the oldest (started in 1920) and most widely read, with a circulation of 260,000. It played an important role in the nationalist movement during Japanese rule, and was eventually banned by the Japanese for almost a decade. From 1945 on the paper consistently supported the Democratic Party and thereby was involved in frequent clashes with the government while the party was in opposition.

There are two English-language dailies, both published in Seoul: *Korean Republic* and the *Korea Times.* The former is a government-subsidized paper and the latter, affiliated with *Han'guk Ilbo,* is independent.

The two major wire services are *Haptong* (Korean Pacific Press) and *Tongyang* (Oriental Press), both of which have nation-wide networks and also distribute AP, UP and other foreign news service reports. In both radio and television, the government-sponsored Korean Broadcasting System (KBS) occupies the predominant position. There are also a few small private radio and television stations.

TABLE 19.   Mass Media

(a) Books published (Number of titles)

1960	1,618
1961	1,412
1962	3,720

(b) Daily newspapers (1962)

Total number	34
Circulation total	1,500,000
Copy per 1,000 of population	57

(c) Radio and television broadcasting (number of receivers estimated)

Radio	1948	88,000
	1960	781,000
	1961	1,158,000
	1962	1,579,000
Television	1961	20,000

SOURCE: UNESCO, in UN *Statistical Yearbook,* 1963, pp. 668-685.

E. The Economy

1. SOURCES

Reliable statistical data is presented with English explanation in the following serials, from which the data given below have been drawn unless otherwise indicated:

South Korean Government Serials:

Economic Statistic Yearbook (Seoul: Bank of Korea)
Economic Survey (Seoul: Economic Planning Board)
Korea Statistical Yearbook (Seoul: Economic Planning Board)
Monthly Review (Seoul: Korean Reconstruction Bank)
Monthly Statistical Review (Seoul: Bank of Korea)
Monthly Statistics of Korea (Seoul: Economic Planning Board)

United Nations Serials:

Demographic Yearbook (New York: Statistical Office of the United Nations)
Economic Bulletin for Asia and the Far East (New York: ECAFE, United Nations)
Monthly Bulletin of Statistics (New York: Statistical Office of the United Nations)
Statistical Yearbook (New York: Statistical Office of the United Nations)

2. POPULATION

TABLE 20.   Estimates of Mid-Year Population (in thousands)

1946	19,369
1947	19,886
1948	20,027
1949	20,208
1950	20,513
1951	20,671
1952	21,144
1953	21,440
1954	21,796
1955	21,526
1956	22,017
1957	22,651
1958	23,303
1959	23,975
1960	24,665
1961	25,375
1962	26,520
1963	27,277

SOURCE: *UN Demographic Yearbook, 1962; 1963*, pp. 154-5.

3. PRODUCTIVITY

TABLE 21. Gross National Product

	1953	1954	1955	1956	1957	1958	1959	1960	1961	1962
At current market price (billion *won*)	38.94	56.67	95.02	121.98	162.99	172.08	185.45	210.71	241.41	281.48
Index (1953=100)	100.0	145.5	244.0	313.3	418.6	441.9	476.2	541.1	620.0	722.9
Annual increase (%)	—	45.5	67.7	28.4	33.6	5.6	7.8	13.6	14.6	15.9
At 1955 constant prices (billion *won*)	86.85	91.35	95.02	95.28	103.53	110.70	116.48	118.89	123.04	125.77
Index (1953=100)	100.0	105.2	109.4	109.7	119.2	127.5	134.1	136.9	141.7	144.8
Growth rates (%)	—	5.2	4.0	0.3	8.7	7.0	5.2	2.1	3.5	2.3

SOURCE: *Monthly Statistical Review*, February 1946, p. 6; *Economic Statistics Yearbook*, 1964, pp. 54-55.

TABLE 22. Index of Industrial Production (1960 = 100)

Year	Total	Mining	Manufacturing	Electricity
1954	43.0	23.9	47.0	53.0
1955	51.4	29.8	56.8	51.8
1956	62.9	38.6	68.7	65.9
1957	72.6	52.2	77.2	77.9
1958	80.0	54.7	85.5	89.0
1959	91.8	76.1	95.1	99.3
1960	100.0	100.0	100.0	100.0
1961	105.7	113.4	104.3	104.3
1962	123.5	134.6	121.8	116.5
1963	139.8	153.6	137.8	130.1

SOURCE: *Monthly Statistics of Korea*, October-November 1964, pp. 4-5.

TABLE 23. Index of Agricultural Production (1952/53-1956/57 = 100)

1952/53	86
1953/54	105
1954/55	104
1955/56	106
1956/57	99
1957/58	109
1958/59	113
1959/60	114
1960/61	116
1961/62	120

SOURCE: *Economic Survey of Asia and the Far East*, 1962, p. 192.

TABLE 24.   The Five-Year Plan 1962-1966

(a) Major indicators of the plan

	Base Year (A) (1960)	Target Year (B) (1966)	B/A (%)
Gross National Product (1961 prices; billion *won*)	233.27	326.91	140.8
Private expenditures (1961 prices; billion *won*)	199.51	235.01	117.8
Total capital formation (1961 prices; billion *won*)	31.39	74.36	236.9
Government expenditures (1961 prices; billion *won*)	37.06	49.83	134.5
Total population	24,694,000	29,185,000	118.2
Labor force	10,394,000	11,868,000	114.2
Employment	7,877,000	10,111,000	128.3
Per-capita income (1961 prices; thousand *won*)	9.41	11.20	119.0

(b) Growth rate and composition ratio of G.N.P.

Industry	Base Year (1960) Growth Rate	Comp. (%)	Initial Year (1962) Growth Rate	Comp. (%)	Target Year (1966) Growth Rate	Comp. (%)	Five-Year growth (%)
Primary	0.9	36.0	5.3	37.1	6.2	34.8	35.8
Secondary	4.3	18.2	11.1	19.4	17.3	26.1	101.9
Tertiary	2.9	45.8	3.8	43.5	4.8	39.1	20.3
Total	2.4	100.0	5.7	100.0	8.3	100.0	40.8

SOURCE: *Korean Affairs*, March-April 1962, pp. 13-16.

4. FOREIGN TRADE
(Import figures include foreign economic aid financed imports.)

TABLE 25. Summary of Exports and Imports (in thousands of U.S. dollars)

Year	Exports	Imports
1952	27,733	214,165
1953	39,585	345,436
1954	24,246	243,327
1955	17,966	341,415
1956	24,595	386,063
1957	22,202	442,174
1958	16,451	378,165
1959	19,812	303,807
1960	32,827	343,527
1961	40,878	316,142
1962	54,813	421,782
1963	86,803	560,273

SOURCE: *Economic Statistical Yearbook, 1964,* p. 285.

TABLE 26. Composition of Imports (percentages)

Year	Consumer Goods		Materials Chiefly for Consumption Goods	Materials Chiefly for Capital Goods	Capital Goods
	Food	Others			
1955	5.2	12.4	42.4	17.3	22.7
1956	11.5	11.5	41.4	17.0	18.5
1957	24.7	10.3	36.6	13.7	14.7
1958	17.6	9.2	41.6	16.0	15.6
1959	9.4	8.9	51.3	12.7	17.9
1960	9.6	15.0	50.1	9.0	16.2
1961	13.4	10.8	47.2	11.4	17.2

SOURCE: *Economic Survey of Asia and the Far East,* 1962, p. 209.

5. FOREIGN ECONOMIC AID

TABLE 27. Summary of Foreign Economic Aid and Supplies Received (in thousands of U.S. dollars)

| Year | Total | USA | | | UNKRA |
		AID*	Food for Peace†	Other	
1945	4,934	—	—	4,934	—
1946	49,496	—	—	49,496	
1947	175,371	—	—	175,371	
1948	179,593	—	—	179,593	
1949	116,509	23,806	—	92,703	
1950	58,706	49,330	—	9,376	
1951	106,542	31,972	—	74,448	122
1952	161,327	3,824	—	155,534	1,969
1953	194,170	5,803	—	158,787	29,580
1954	153,925	82,437	—	50,191	21,297
1955	236,707	205,815	—	8,711	22,181
1956	326,705	271,049	32,955	311	22,370
1957	382,893	323,268	45,522	—	14,103
1958	321,272	265,629	47,896	—	7,747
1959	222,204	208,297	11,436	—	2,471
1960	245,394	225,237	19,913	—	244
1961	199,245	154,319	44,926	—	—
1962	232,310	165,002	67,308	—	—
1963	216,483	119,659	96,824	—	—
Total	3,367,303	2,015,788	269,956	959,475	122,084

* Includes ECA, SEC and ICA.
† Under PL 480.
SOURCE: *Economic Statistical Yearbook, 1961*, p. 192; *Monthly Statistical Review*, August 1963, p. 72; and *Korean Annual—1964*, p. 579.

6. SECURITY

TABLE 28. Republic of Korea Defense Expenditures (in billions of won)

Fiscal Year	1959	1960	1961	1962	1963 budget	1964 budget
(A) Expenditures of General Account	30.94	35.14	46.33	68.34	51.48	50.92
(B) Expenditures by Ministry of National Defense	13.92	14.707	16.60	20.47	21.43	22.77
Defense as % of total	45.0	41.9	35.8	29.9	41.6	44.7

SOURCE: *Korea Statistical Yearbook 1964*, p. 328.

TABLE 29. United States Military Assistance to the Republic of Korea (in millions of U.S. dollars)

Fiscal Year	Assistance
1961	230
1962	180
1963	160
1964	141
1965	114

SOURCE: Data for 1961-62 in *Korean Annual—1964*, p. 173; for 1963-65 in *The New York Times*, January 5, 1965.

III. THE DEMOCRATIC PEOPLE'S REPUBLIC OF KOREA

A. Government Structure

The Democratic People's Republic of Korea was established in North Korea in September 1948. Born as a result of "nation-wide" general elections, the new government was essentially the outgrowth of "people's committees" that had acted as administrative bodies during the Soviet military occupation (1945–1948).

The Supreme People's Assembly, a unicameral national legislature, is the highest organ of the state. Its 213 members are elected for four-year terms and the Assembly meets twice a year. Most of the Assembly's work is carried out by its Standing Committee, the Chairman of which acts as chief of state.

The Council of Ministers, which is appointed by the Supreme People's Assembly, is the highest administrative organ and its chairman, the Premier, is the chief executive. The Council has, in addition to the Premier, Deputy Premiers and a number of Ministers. The core of the Council is its Standing Committee, composed of the Premier and Deputy Premiers.

The Supreme Court and the *Supreme Procurate* are the highest bodies in their respective fields. Their chief officers are appointed by the Supreme People's Assembly.

B. Political Parties

The Korean Workers' Party, established in 1946, is the ruling party and its membership is estimated at well over 1 million. (The last announced figure is 1,178,000 for 1956.) The Party Congress convenes every four years, electing a Central Committee (71 members and 45 candidate members), which is the Party's executive body. The locus of power, however, is the Standing Committee of the Central Committee (at present, 11 members and 4 candidates), whose members concurrently occupy important posts in the government. The Chairman of the Standing Committee is Premier Kim Il-sung.

The North Korean government is essentially a one-party dictatorship of the Workers' Party but two other "bourgeois" parties are allowed to maintain a nominal existence, namely, the *North Korean Democratic Party* (established in 1945) and the *Ch'ŏndo-kyo Ch'ŏngwu Party* (established in 1946). Remnants of parties organized in North Korea after World War II but before the Communist take-over, these parties are kept, if in name only, as a façade that ostensibly justifies the name "People's Democracy."

The Democratic Front for Unification of the Fatherland, established in 1949, is an organization specifically set up for the purpose of mobilizing both Communist and non-Communist organizations for united action to promote the unification of Korea. Political and social leaders in North Korea who had once been active in South Korea have been among the nominal officers of the Front, which is in fact manipulated by the Workers' Party.

C. Principal Personalities

Kim Il-sung (1912-   ). Premier since 1948, he is also Chairman of the Central Committee of the Korean Workers' (Communist) Party. He is a long-time resident of Manchuria, went to school there, and eventually became an anti-Japanese guerrilla leader, having become a Communist in 1931. Returning to Korea in 1945, he quickly emerged as an important Communist leader in North Korea and has remained in power ever since.

Ch'oe Yŏng-kŏn (1903-   ). Chairman of the Standing Committee of the Supreme People's Assembly, he is the "president" of North Korea. A graduate of a Chinese military academy, he, like Kim, was long active in the Communist anti-Japanese guerrilla forces in Manchuria. After his return to North Korea in 1945, he became head of the police organization and eventually served as Defense Minister before assuming his present post.

D. Mass Organizations

The General Federation of Trade Unions, organized in 1945, now consists of nine industrial union organizations on the national level, with a total membership of around 600,000.

135

The Korean Democratic Youth League, organized in 1946, is the youth branch of the Korean Workers' Party, with a membership of 1.8 million. In addition, 1.5 million children hold junior membership in the League.

The Korean Democratic Women's League, organized in 1945, is the major national women's organization; its members number over 2 million.

E. Mass Communications Media

There are two major daily papers, Nodong Shinmun and Minju Chosun, the former an organ of the Workers' Party Central Committee and the latter an organ of the Council of Ministers. The government wire service is Chosun Chungang Tongshin (Korean Central News Agency) and radio broadcasting is likewise under government control.

TABLE 30. Mass Media

Year	1946	1949	1953	1956	1957	1958
Newspapers						
Number	23	31	22	31	29	31
Circulation (1,000)	71,427	206,413	104,103	174,100	185,568	225,188
Magazines						
Number	29	46	18	51	55	61
Circulation (1,000)	444	5,443	2,862	18,123	25,396	29,052
Books						
Titles	213	587	414	846	926	1,392
Copies printed (1,000)	950	5,751	4,305	14,423	12,321	35,623

SOURCE: Korea (DPRK) Chosŏn Chungang T'ongsin Sa, Chosŏn Chungang Yon'gam 1959, p. 338.

F. The Economy

TABLE 31. Population and Vital Statistics

Year	Population in 1,000's	Births per 1,000	Deaths per 1,000	Increase per 1,000
1949	9,083	41.2	18.7	22.5
1953	8,560	25.1	18.1	7.0
1956	9,383	31.0	17.6	13.4
1960	10,789	38.5	10.5	28.0
1961	11,061	36.7	11.5	25.2
1962	11,393	41.1	10.8	30.0

SOURCE: Nissen Bōeki-kai, in *Tōitsu Chōsen nenkan, 1964* (Tokyo: Tōitsu Chōsen Shimbunsha, 1965), p. 735; U.N. *Demographic Yearbook, 1962*, pp. 136-137, for population of 1949, 1953 and 1956; population for 1961 and 1962 calculated from increase data.

TABLE 32. Population by Social Group (percentages)

	1946	1949	1953	1954	1956	1957	1958
Total	100	100	100	100	100	100	100
Industrial workers	12.5	19.0	21.2	25.7	27.3	28.7	31.7
Workers in farm cooperatives	—	—	—	17.1	40.0	49.9	49.8
Farmers	74.1	69.3	66.4	44.2	16.6	3.2	—
Others	13.4	11.7	12.4	13.0	16.1	18.2	18.5

SOURCE: *Chosŏn Chungang Yon'gam, 1959*, p. 322.

ABLE 33. State Investment in Capital Construction (at 1950 estimated prices)

	1949	1954	1955	1956	1957	1958	
Total	6,660	24,831	29,349	26,402	27,136	34,122	(million *won*)
Productive construction	4,656 (69.9)	17,578 (70.8)	21,963 (74.8)	19,397 (73.5)	19,662 (72.5)	25,390 (74.4)	(percentages)
Non-productive construction	2,004 (30.1)	7,253 (29.2)	7,386 (25.2)	7,005 (26.5)	7,474 (27.5)	8,733 (25.6)	

SOURCE: *Chosŏn Chungang Yon'gam, 1959*, pp. 332-33.

137

TABLE 34. Index of National Income (1946 = 100)

Year	Index
1946	100
1949	209
1953	145
1956	319
1960	683
1961	810

SOURCE: Nissen Bōeki-kai, in *Tōitsu Chōsen nenkan*, 1964, p. 734.

TABLE 35. Composition of Social Product by Sector (in percentages)

Sector	1946	1949	1953	1956	1960	1961
Total	100.0	100.0	100.0	100.0	100.0	100.0
Industry	23.2	35.6	30.7	40.1	57.1	56.3
Agriculture	59.1	40.6	41.6	25.6	23.6	24.8
Transportation and communication	1.6	2.9	3.7	4.0	2.2	1.9
Fundamental construction	—	7.2	14.9	12.3	8.7	6.7
Commerce	12.0	9.4	6.0	10.8	6.0	8.2
Other	4.1	4.3	3.1	6.2	2.4	2.1

SOURCE: *Tōitsu Chōsen nenkan*, 1964, p. 734.

TABLE 36. Index of Industrial Production (1946 = 100)

	1953	1954	1955	1956	1957	1958
General	100	151	224	285	412	564
Means of production	100	189	308	405	592	798
Consumer goods	100	128	174	209	299	417

SOURCE: *Chosŏn Chungang Yon'gam*, 1959, p. 325.

TABLE 37. Agricultural Production:
Gross Tonnage of Grain Production (1,000 tons)

1944	1946	1947	1948	1949	1951	1952
2,417	1,898	2,069	2,668	2,654	2,260	2,450

1953	1954	1955	1956	1957	1958
2,327	2,320	2,340	2,873	3,201	3,700

SOURCE: *Chosŏn Chungang Yon'gam*, 1959, p. 332.

TABLE 38. North Korean Trade with Japan (in thousands of U.S. dollars)

Year	Exports to Japan	Imports from Japan	Total
1956	506.80	92.96	599.76
1957	2,005.08	2,129.96	4,135.04
1958	1,927.80	2,119.88	4,047.68
1959	768.04	2,831.08	3,599.12
1960	3,089.80	1,852.48	4,942.28
1961	3,975.72	4,938.36	8,914.08
1961*	3,975.72	9,279.76	13,255.48
1962	3,984.96	4,657.52	8,642.48
1963	8,914.36	5,678.68	14,593.04
1963*	8,914.36	10,845.52	19,759.88

* Includes value of Japanese exports to North Korea shipped indirectly via Hong Kong.

SOURCE: Nissen Bōeki-kai, in *Tōitsu Chōsen nenkan*, 1946 (Tokyo: Tōitsu Chōsen Shimbunsha, 1965), p. 427.

BIBLIOGRAPHY

A. Japan

1. General

Beasley, William G. *The Modern History of Japan*. New York: Praeger, 1963.
Borton, Hugh, *Japan Between East and West*. New York: Harper, 1957.
————. *Japan's Modern Century*. New York: The Ronald Press Co., 1955.
Hall, Robert B., Jr. *Japan: Industrial Power of Asia*. Princeton: D. Van Nostrand Co., 1963.
Japanese National Commission for UNESCO. *Japan: Its Land, People and Culture*. Tokyo: Ministry of Finance, 1958.
Keene, Donald. *Living Japan*. Garden City: Doubleday, 1959.
Olson, Lawrence. *Dimensions of Japan*. New York: American Universities Field Staff, 1963.
Reischauer, Edwin O. *Japan: Past and Present*. New York: Alfred A. Knopf, 1956.
————. *The United States and Japan*. Rev. ed. Cambridge: Harvard University Press, 1957.
Sansom, George. *The Western World and Japan: A Study in the Interaction of European and Asiatic Cultures*. New York: Alfred A. Knopf, 1949.
Storry, Richard. *A History of Modern Japan*. Harmondsworth: Penguin Books, 1960.
Tiedemann, Arthur. *Modern Japan: A Brief History*. 2nd ed. Princeton: D. Van Nostrand Co., 1962.
Tsunoda, Ryusaku, William Theodore DeBary, and Donald Keene (comps.). *Sources of the Japanese Tradition*. New York: Columbia University Press, 1958.
Webb, Herschel. *An Introduction to Japan*. 2nd ed. New York: Columbia University Press, 1957.
Yanaga, Chitoshi. *Japan Since Perry*. New York: McGraw-Hill Book Co., 1949.

2. Politics

Burks, Ardath W. *The Government of Japan*. New York: Thomas Y. Crowell Co., 1964.
Colbert, Evelyn S. *The Left Wing in Japanese Politics*. New York: Institute of Pacific Relations, 1952.

Cole, Allan B. *Japanese Society and Politics: The Impact of Social Stratification and Mobility on Politics*. Boston: Boston University, 1956.

——. *Political Tendencies of Japanese in Small Enterprises*. New York: Institute of Pacific Relations, 1959.

Ike, Nobutaka. *Japanese Politics: An Introductory Survey*. New York: Alfred A. Knopf, 1956.

Japan. Ministry of Justice. *The Constitution of Japan and Criminal Statutes*. Tokyo: Government Printing Bureau, 1958.

Kawai, Kazuo. *Japan's American Interlude*. Chicago: University of Chicago Press, 1960.

Kurzman, Dan. *Kishi and Japan: The Search for the Sun*. New York: Ivan Obolensky, 1960.

Langer, Paul F. "The Japanese Communist Party between Mosccow and Peking." In *Communist Strategies in Asia*, edited by A. Doak Barnett. New York: Praeger, 1963, Pp. 63-100.

McNelly, Theodore. *Contemporary Government of Japan*. Boston: Houghton Mifflin Co., 1963.

Maki, John M. *Court and Constitution in Japan*. Seattle: University of Washington Press, 1964.

——. *Government and Politics in Japan: The Road to Democracy*. New York: Praeger, 1962.

Martin, Edwin M. *The Allied Occupation of Japan*. New York: American Institute of Pacific Relations, 1948.

Maruyama, Masao. *Thought and Behavior in Modern Japanese Politics*. New York: Oxford University Press, 1963.

Morris, Ivan. *Nationalism and the Right Wing in Japan: A Study of Post-War Trends*. London: Oxford University Press, 1960.

Quigley, Harold S., and John E. Turner. *The New Japan: Government and Politics*. Minneapolis: University of Minnesota Press, 1956.

Scalapino, Robert A., and Junnosuke Masumi. *Parties and Politics in Contemporary Japan*. Berkeley and Los Angeles: University of California Press, 1962.

SCAP. Government Section. *The Political Reorientation of Japan*. 2 vols. Washington: Government Printing Office, 1949.

Swearingen, Rodger, and Paul Langer. *Red Flag in Japan: International Communism in Action, 1919-1951*. Cambridge: Harvard University Press, 1952.

Von Mehren, Arthur T. (ed.). *Law in Japan: The Legal Order in a Changing Society*. Cambridge: Harvard University Press, 1963.

Whitney, Courtney. *MacArthur: His Rendezvous with History*. New York: Alfred A. Knopf, 1956.

Wildes, Harry Emerson. *Typhoon in Tokyo: The Occupation and Its Aftermath*. New York: The Macmillan Co., 1954.

Yanaga, Chitoshi. *Japanese People and Politics*. New York: John Wiley and Sons, 1956.

Yoshida, Shigeru. *The Yoshida Memoirs: The Story of Japan in Crisis*. Boston: Houghton Mifflin Co., 1962.

3. Foreign Relations

Cohen, Bernard. *The Political Process and Foreign Policy: The Making of the Japanese Peace Settlement*. Princeton: Princeton University Press, 1957.

Dunn, Frederick S. *Peace-making and the Settlement with Japan*. Princeton: Princeton University Press, 1963.

Japan Association of International Law (ed.). *Japan and the United Nations*. New York: Manhattan Publishing Co., 1958.

Mendel, Douglas H. *The Japanese People and Foreign Policy: A Study of Public Opinion in Post-Treaty Japan.* Berkeley and Los Angeles: University of California Press, 1961.
Morley, James W. "Japan's Image of the Soviet Union, 1952-61," *Pacific Affairs,* Vol. XXXV, No. 1 (Spring, 1962), pp. 51-58.
―――. "Japan's Position in Asia," *Journal of International Affairs,* Vol. XVII, No. 2 (1963), pp. 142-154.
―――. "Japan's Security Policy in Transition," *Current History,* April, 1964.
―――. *Soviet and Chinese Communist Policies Toward Japan, 1950-1957: A Comparison.* New York: Institute of Pacific Relations, 1958.
―――. "The Soviet-Japanese Peace Declaration," *Political Science Quarterly,* Vol. LXXII, No. 3 (September, 1957), pp. 370-379.
Scalapino, Robert A. "The Foreign Policy of Modern Japan." In *Foreign Policy in World Politics,* edited by Roy C. Macridis. 2d ed. Englewood Cliffs: Prentice-Hall, 1962. Pp. 225-266.
―――. "The United States and Japan." In *The United States and the Far East,* edited by William L. Thorp for the American Assembly. 2nd ed. Englewood Cliffs: Prentice-Hall, 1962. Chapter 1.
Seki, Yoshihiko. "The Foreign Policy of Japan." In *Foreign Policies in a World of Change,* edited by Joseph E. Black and Kenneth W. Thompson. New York: Harper, 1963. Pp. 517-546.

4. Social and Economic Conditions

Abegglen, James C. *The Japanese Factory.* Glencoe: Free Press, 1958.
Anderson, Ronald S. *Japan: Three Epochs of Modern Education.* Washington: Government Printing Office, 1959.
Battistini, Lawrence H. *The Postwar Student Struggle in Japan.* Tokyo: Charles E. Tuttle, 1956.
Beardsley, Richard K., John W. Hall and Robert E. Ward. *Village Japan.* Chicago: University of Chicago Press, 1959.
Bennett, John W., and Ishino Iwao. *Paternalism in the Japanese Economy.* Minneapolis: University of Minnesota Press, 1963.
Cohen, Jerome B. *Japan's Economy in War and Reconstruction.* Minneapolis: University of Minnesota Press, 1949.
―――. *Japan's Postwar Economy.* Bloomington: Indiana University Press, 1958.
Dore, R. P. *City Life in Japan: A Study of a Tokyo Ward.* Berkeley and Los Angeles: University of California Press, 1958.
―――. *Land Reform in Japan.* New York: Oxford University Press, 1959.
Fukutake, Tadashi. *Man and Society in Japan.* Tokyo: University of Tokyo Press, 1962.
Gibney, Frank. *Five Gentlemen of Japan: The Portrait of a Nation's Character.* New York: Farrar, Straus and Young, 1953.
Levine, Solomon B. *Industrial Relations in Postwar Japan.* Urbana: University of Illinois Press, 1958.
Matsumoto, Yoshiharu Scott. *Contemporary Japan: The Individual and the Group.* Philadelphia: American Philosophical Society, 1960.
Okochi, Kazuo. *Labor in Japan.* Tokyo: Government Printing Bureau, 1958.
Plath, David W. *After Hours: Modern Japan and the Search for Enjoyment.* Berkeley: University of California Press, 1964.
Stoetzel, Jean. *Without the Chrysanthemum and the Sword.* New York: Columbia University Press, 1955.

Tauber, Irene. *The Population of Japan.* Princeton: Princeton University Press, 1958.
Vining, Elizabeth Gray. *Windows for the Crown Prince.* Philadelphia: J. P. Lippincott Co., 1952.
Vogel, Ezra F. *Japan's New Middle Class.* Berkeley: University of California Press, 1963.
Whittemore, Edward P. *The Press in Japan Today.* Columbia: University of South Carolina Press, 1961.

5. Serials (See also "Sources" under "The Economy")

Asian Survey (monthly), Berkeley: University of California.
Contemporary Japan (quarterly), Tokyo: Foreign Affairs Association of Japan.
Economic Bulletin for Asia and Far East (quarterly), New York: United Nations.
Far Eastern Economic Review (weekly), Hong Kong: Far Eastern Economic Review, Ltd.
Information Bulletin (annual), Tokyo: Ministry of Foreign Affairs.
Japan Annual, Tokyo: Institute of World Economy.
Japan Annual of International Affairs, Tokyo: Japan Institute of International Affairs.
Japan Annual of International Law, Tokyo: International Law Association.
Japan Annual of Law and Politics, Tokyo: Science Council of Japan.
Japan Economic Yearbook, Tokyo: Oriental Economist.
Japan Labor Yearbook, Tokyo: Ministry of Labor.
Japan Quarterly, Tokyo: Asahi Shimbun Publishing Co.
Japan Reports (bi-monthly), New York: Japanese Consulate-General.
Journal of Asian Studies (quarterly), Ann Arbor: Association of Asian Studies.
Journal of Social and Political Ideas in Japan (published in April, August and December), Tokyo: Center for Japanese Social and Political Studies.
Orient/West (bi-monthly), Tokyo: Orient/West, Inc.
Pacific Affairs (quarterly), Vancouver: University of British Columbia.

* * *

Asahi Evening News (daily), Tokyo: Asahi Shimbunsha.
Japan Economic Journal (weekly), Tokyo: Nihon Keizai Shimbunsha.
Japan Times (daily), Tokyo: Japan Times.
Japan Times Weekly (international edition), Tokyo: Japan Times.
Mainichi Daily News (monthly international edition), Tokyo: Mainichi Shimbunsha.
Mainichi Daily News, Tokyo: Mainichi Shimbunsha.
Yomiuri (daily), Tokyo: Yomiuri Shimbunsha.

B. South Korea

1. Books and Articles

Allen, Richard (pseud.). *C. L. Korea's Syngman Rhee.* Rutland: Tuttle, 1960.
Berger, Carl. *The Korea Knot.* Philadelphia: University of Pennsylvania, 1957.
Chung, Kyung Cho. *Korea Tomorrow.* New York: Macmillan, 1956.
———. *New Korea.* New York: Macmillan, 1962.
Goodrich, Leland M. *Korea: A Study of United States Policy in the United Nations.* New York: Council on Foreign Relations, 1956.
———. *Korea: Collective Measures Against Aggression.* New York: Carnegie Endowment for International Peace, 1953.

Gordenker, Leon. *The United Nations and the Peaceful Unification of Korea.* The Hague: Martins Nijhoff, 1959.

Hellman, Donald C. "Basic Problems of Japanese-South Korean Relations," *Asian Survey,* Vol. II, no. 3 (May, 1962), pp. 19-24.

Joy, Charles T. *How Communists Negotiate.* New York: Macmillan, 1955.

Korea, Its Land, People and Culture of All Ages. Seoul: Hakwon-sa, 1960.

Korea Annual—1964. Seoul: Hapdong News Agency, 1964.

Lee, Chong-sik. "Japanese-Korean Relations in Perspective," *Pacific Affairs,* Vol. XXXV, no. 4 (Winter, 1962-63), pp. 315-326.

Lyons, Gene M. *Military Policy and Economic Aid: The Korean Case, 1950-1953.* Columbus: Ohio State University Press, 1953.

McCune, George M. *Korea Today.* Cambridge: Harvard University Press, 1950.

McCune, Shannon. *Korea's Heritage.* Rutland: Tuttle, 1956.

———. *The United States and Korea.* In Willard Thorp (ed.), *The United States and the Far East.* Englewood Cliffs: Prentice-Hall, 1962.

Meade, E. Grant. *American Military Government in Korea.* New York: King's Crown Press, 1951.

Min, Byong-ki. "Problems in the Korean-Japanese Relations," *Koreana Quarterly,* Vol. 6, no. 1 (Spring, 1964), pp. 39-45.

O, Chae-gyong. *A Handbook of Korea.* New York: Pageant, 1957.

Oliver, Robert T. *Syngman Rhee.* New York: Dodd, Mead, 1954.

———. *Verdict in Korea.* State College, Pa.: Bald Eagle Press, 1952.

———. *Why War Came in Korea.* New York: Fordham University Press, 1950.

Osgood, Cornelius. *The Koreans and Their Culture.* New York: Ronald Press, 1951.

Pyun, Yung-tai. *Korea: My Country.* Seoul: Council on Korean Affairs, 1962.

———. "On Korea-Japan Relations," *Korean Affairs,* Vol. 1, no. 3 (1962), pp. 280-285.

Reeve, W. D. *The Republic of Korea: A Political and Economic Study.* New York: Oxford University Press, 1963.

Republic of Korea. Economic Planning Board. Bureau of Statistics. *Statistical Handbook of Korea.* Seoul, 1962.

———. Ministry of Reconstruction. *Summary of the First Five-Year Economic Plan, 1962-1966.* Seoul, 1962.

———. Supreme Council for National Reconstruction. Secretariat. *Military Revolution in Korea.* Seoul, 1961.

United States. Department of State. *Korea, 1945 to 1948.* Washington: GPO, 1948.

———. *The Record of Korean Unification, 1943-1960: Narrative Summary with Principal Documents.* Washington: GPO, 1960.

Vatcher, William H. *Panmunjom: The Story of the Korean Armistice.* New York: Praeger, 1958.

Whiting, Allen S. *China Crosses the Yalu.* New York: Macmillan, 1960.

Wint, Guy. *What Happened in Korea.* London: Batchworth Press, 1954.

Yu, Chin-o. "What Prevents the Successful Conclusion of the Korea-Japan Conference?" *Korean Affairs,* Vol. 2 (May/June, 1962), pp. 122-126.

2. Serials (See also "Sources" under "The Economy")

Asian Survey (monthly). Berkeley: University of California, Institute of International Studies.

Asiatic Research Bulletin (monthly). Seoul: Asiatic Research Center, Korea University.

Bulletin. Seoul: Ministry of Foreign Affairs.
Bulletin of the Korean Research Center: A Journal of Social Sciences and Humanities (semi-annual). Seoul: Korean Research Center.
Far Eastern Economic Review (weekly). Hong Kong: Far Eastern Economic Review, Ltd.
Journal of Asiatic Studies (semi-annual). Seoul: Korea University, Asiatic Research Center.
Korea Information Bulletin. Washington: The Korean Embassy.
Korea Journal (monthly). Seoul: Korean National Commission for UNESCO.
Korea Times (daily). Seoul: Korea Times, Inc.
Korea Trade (monthly). Seoul: Korea Trade Promotion Corporation.
Korean Affairs (quarterly). Seoul: Council on Korean Affairs.
Korean Report (monthly; formerly *Korean Survey*). Washington: Korean Information Office.
Korean Republic (daily). Seoul: Korean Republic, Inc.
Koreana Quarterly. Seoul: International Research Center.
Pacific Affairs (quarterly). Vancouver: University of British Columbia.
Press Translations: Korea. Seoul: North Asia Press.
Voice of Korea (monthly). Washington: Korean Affairs Institute.

C. North Korea

There are very few books about the North Korean regime in English. The best are Robert A. Scalapino (ed.), *North Korea Today* (New York: Praeger, 1963) and Philip Rudolph, *North Korea's Political and Economic Structure* (New York: Institute of Pacific Relations, 1959). Glenn D. Paige has an important article in *Communist Strategies in Asia* (New York: Praeger, 1963). Other useful articles are to be found occasionally in *China Quarterly, Foreign Affairs* and particularly in the following serials:

Asian Survey (monthly). Berkeley: Institute of International Studies, University of California.
Korean Affairs (quarterly). Seoul: Council on Korean Affairs.
Pacific Affairs (quarterly). Vancouver: University of British Columbia.

The United States Government publishes a number of useful works. Among them are the translations (mimeographed) from the North Korean press by the Joint Publications Research Service, including series on *Agriculture in North Korea, Economic Report on North Korea, Industrial Development in North Korea, Political Report on North Korea,* and the *Central Yearbook.* In addition, the U. S. Department of State has issued *North Korea: A Case Study in the Technique of Takeover* (Washington: GPO, 1961).
The North Korean Government itself has published through its Foreign Language Publishing House in Pyongyang a number of volumes in English, including *Facts About Korea* (1961), *Korea, 1945–1960* (1960) and *Statistical Returns of National Economy of the Democratic Republic of Korea (1946–60)* (1961), together with a variety of serials in English, the most readily available being:

Korea (an illustrated monthly).
Korea Information Series (pamphlets issued irregularly).
Korea News (three times a month).
Korea Today (monthly).
The People's Korea (a weekly newspaper published in Tokyo).

INDEX

Adachi, Tadashi, 98
Agricultural Cooperative Associations, 20
Agriculture, see Farmers and farming
All-Japan Communications Workers Union, 99
All-Japan Conference of Government Workers Unions, 85
All-Japan Conference of Patriots' Organizations, 88
All-Japan Congress of Trade Unions, see Dōmei Kaigi
All-Japan Farmers Union, 96
All-Japan Federation of Farmers Unions, 86-87
All-Japan Federation of Student Self-Governing Organizations (Zengakuren), 69, 87
All-Japan Seamen's Union, 100
All-Japan Trade Union Congress (Zenrō), 34, 85, 100
Army Club of Japan, 89-90
Asanuma, Inejirō, 35, 72, 88
Ashida, Hitoshi, 29, 69, 83
Asia, Japanese relations with
political, 4-5, 11-15
Korea central to conflicts in, 54
trade, 9-11, 14-15, 106-7
See also specific countries
Ayukawa, Gisuke, 32

Bonin Islands, 3, 7-8, 12
Business associations (Japan), 84-85
leaders, 98-99

Cabinet (Japan), 76
Chamber of Commerce and Industry of Japan, 84-85, 93, 98

Chang Myŏn (John M. Chang), 43, 50-51, 117
life, 124
Chayu Minju-dang, 120-21
Chiang Kai-shek, 38
China, Japan and , 65, 70, 73
defense against Communism, 15-18
Nationalist China, 12-13, 70
Sino-Japanese War, 8, 55
trade, 4, 9, 16-17, 70-73, 106-7
China, Korean political relations with, 40, 55-56, 64, 115-17
See also Taiwan
Cho Bong-am, 55
Ch'oe Yŏng-kŏn, 135
Ch'ŏndo-kyo Ch'ŏngwu Party (N. Korea), 135
Chōsōren, 64
Chou Hung-chin, 73
Chronology of key events
Japan, 68-73
Korea, 115-18
Chung-hee Park, see Park Chung-hee
Churitsu Rōren, 86
Chuseiren Political Federation of Medium and Small Enterprise, 32
Civil Rule Party (ROK), 45, 120
Clan Government Party of Japan, see Kōmeitō
Communications media
Japanese, 90-92
North Korean, 136
South Korean, 125-26
Communism
Japanese, 16, 27-28, 32-34, 63, 69, 77, 87, 97-98

147

Fujiwara, Hirotatsu, 21-22
Fukuda, Takeo, 24, 93

General Council of Trade Unions of Japan, *see Sōhyō*
General Federation of Korean Residents in Japan, 64
General Federation of Labor Unions of Japan (*Sōdōmei*), 85, 97
Gensuikyō, 34, 89
Germany, 23, 91-92, 102
Great Britain, 23, 91–92, 102
Green Breeze Society, 78

Hatoyama, Ichirō, 25, 71, 83, 94-95
Heimin Gakuren, 87
Higashikuni, Prince, 68, 83
Hirohito, *see* Emperor of Japan
Hō Chōng, 117, 122, 124
Hoantai, 70-71, 110

Ikeda, Hayato, 24, 72-73, 83, 93
Inagaki, Heitarō, 98
International Military Tribunal, 68-69
Ishibashi, Tanzan, 25, 71-72, 83
Ishida, Hakuei, 94
Ishii, Mitsujirō, 24-25, 94
Ishizaka, Taizō, 98
Iwai, Akira, 99
Iwasa, Yoshizane, 98

Japan Society (Council) Against Atomic and Hydrogen Bombs, 34, 89
Japan United Congress of Labor, *see Dōmei Kaigi*
Japan-U. S. Administrative Agreement (1952), 70-71
Japan-U. S. Security Pact (1960), *see* Treaty of Mutual Cooperation and Security
Japanese-Korean relations, *see* Korean-Japanese relations
Jieitai (Self-Defense Forces), 6-7, 71, 110-12
Jimintō, *see* Conservative political party of Japan
Jiseidō, 88
Jiyu-Minshutō, *see* Conservative political party of Japan

Junta rule in Korea, 43-45, 117-19, 121

Kaiin, 100
Kaikōsha, 89-90
Katayama, Tetsu, 29, 69, 83, 97
Kawakami, Jōtarō, 27, 96
Kawashima, Shōjirō, 24-25, 94
Keisatsu yobitai (National Police Reserve), 4, 7, 69, 110
Keizai Dantai Rengōkai (*Keidanren*), 20, 84
Keizai Dōyȳkai, 85
Kikawada, Kazutaka, 98-99
Kim Chong-p'il, Brig. Gen., 46, 118, 125
Kim Il-sung, 39, 54, 115, 135
Kim Ku, 55
Kim Kyu-sik, 54-55
Kishi, Nobusuke, 8, 24, 65, 72, 83
  life, 94
  wounded, 88
Kōmeitō, 73, 78, 89
Kōno, Ichirō, 25, 29, 94-95
Korean Democratic Party (ROK), 121
Korean Democratic Women's League, 136
Korean Democratic Youth League, 136
Korean Independence Party (ROK), 121
Korean-Japanese relations
  educational, 49, 51
  political, 8, 11-12, 16, 35, 38, 72-73, 115-18
  U. S. in, 54-66
  trade, 57-58, 62, 64-65, 139
Korean Nationalist Party, (ROK), 121
Korean War, 2, 11, 40, 47-48, 52
  armistice, 71, 115-16
  start, 69, 115
Kubota, Kanichiro, 60
Kungmin-ui-dang, 120-21
Kurile Islands, 3, 11, 17
Kuroda, Hisao, 27
Kyōyūren, 90

Labor Party (ROK), 54-55
Labor-Farmer Party of Japan, 27, 96
Labor unions

Labor unions (continued)
Japanese, 30-32, 34, 64, 68, 85-87, 99-100
North Korean, 135
See also specific unions
Leftist political parties of Japan, see Progressive political parties of Japan
Liberal Party (ROK), 42-43, 121
Liberal-Democratic Party
Japanese, see Conservative political party of Japan
ROK, 120-21
Liberal-Republican Party (ROK), 118
Liberal Youth League of Japan, 88
Lyuh Un-hyong, 54-55

MacArthur, Gen. Douglas, 68, 70
Matsumura, Kenzō, 25
Middle class in Japan, 31-32
Middle Eastern–Japanese trade, 106-7
Miki, Bukichi, 29
Miki, Takeo, 25, 95
Minjŏng-dang (Civil Rule Party), 45, 120-21
Minju-dang, see Democratic Party (ROK)
Minju Konghwa-dang, see Democratic Republican Party (ROK)
Minseidō, 33, 87
Minshatō, 77
Minshu-Shakaitō, 77
Miyamoto, Kenji, 97
Mizuno, Shigeo, 99
Mutual Cooperation and Security Treaty, see Treaty of Mutual Cooperation and Security
Mutual Defense Assistance Agreement (Japan–U. S., 1954), 6-7, 56, 71, 112
Mutual Defense Treaty (N. Korea–Japan, 1961), 56
Mutual Security Pact (U. S.–ROK, 1953), 116

Nakaji, Kumazō, 100
Nakasone, Yasuhiro, 95
Narita, Tomomi, 27, 33, 96
National Alliance of Textile Workers Union (Japan), 100
National Association of Agricultural Cooperatives of Japan, 86

National Association of Industrial Unions of Japan, 86
National Cooperative Party of Japan, 95
National Defense Council of Japan, 71, 111-12
National Farmers League of Japan, 87
National Farmers Party of Japan, 95-96
National Federation of Farmers of Japan, 87
National Police Reserve of Japan, 4, 7, 69, 110
National Railway Workers Union (Japan), 99
National Security Law (ROK, 1958), 43
Navy Club of Japan, 89-90
Newspapers, see Communications media
Nichinō, 86
Nihon Bōekikai, 85
Nihon Keieisha Dantai Remmei (Nikkeiren), 20, 84
Nihon Kyōsantō, see Communism (Japanese)
Nihon Shōkō Kaigisho (Nisshō), 84-85
Niin Kurabu, 78
Nikkeiren, 20, 84
Nishio, Suehiro, 29-30, 72, 77, 97
Nisshō, 84-85
Nōkyō, 86
Nomizo, Masaru, 27
North Korean Democratic Party, 135
North Korean Workers Party, 39-41, 134-36
Nosaka, Sanzō, 97-98

Okinawa, 7-8, 12, 73
Ono, Bamboku, 22
Ōta, Kaoru, 99

Park Chung-hee, 44-46, 55, 117-19, 122
life, 124
U. S. pressure on, 57
Party of the People (ROK), 120-21
Peace (Rhee) Line, 59, 70, 115
Peace movement in Japan, 34, 71, 89
Philippines, 13